D1523261

A Civilian Occupation

THE POLITICS OF ISRAELI ARCHITECTURE

Babel

VERSO

pages 2–9: Derech Ha'avot [Hebrew: The Way of the Patriarchs], near Elazar, Bethlehem region / Shaked, Jenin region / Pisgat Ze'ev and the Palestinian village of Anata, Jerusalem / Kfar Edummim (on the left) and Nofei Prat, Jericho region
photographs: Milutin Labudovic for Peace Now (Shalom Achshav), 2002

A CIVILIAN OCCUPATION

THE POLITICS
OF ISRAELI ARCHITECTURE

EDITED BY:
RAFI SEGAL
EYAL WEIZMAN

DESIGNED BY:
DAVID TARTAKOVER

DANIEL BAUER
B'TSELEM
MERON BENVENISTI
ZVI EFRAT
NADAV HAREL
MIKI KRATSMAN
MILUTIN LABUDOVIC
GIDEON LEVY

ILAN POTASH
SHARON ROTBARD
RAFI SEGAL
EFRAT SHVILY
ERAN TAMIR-TAWIL
EYAL WEIZMAN
PAVEL WOLBERG
OREN YIFTACHEL

Babel
Tel Aviv

VERSO
London · New York

This book is a revised edition of
A Civilian Occupation: The Politics of Israeli Architecture
("The banned catalog")
First published by the Israeli Association of United Architects (IAUA)
for the Union Internationale des Architectes (UIA) Congress in Berlin, July 2002

10 9 8 7 6 5 4 3 2 1

Babel
Architectures series editor, Sharon Rotbard
26 Ralbag Street, Tel Aviv-Jaffa 66178, Israel
www.babel.co.il

Verso
UK: 6 Meard Street, London W1F 0EG
USA: 180 Varick Street, New York, NY 10014-4606
www.versobooks.com
Verso is the imprint of New Left Books

ISBN 1-85984-549-5

British Library Cataloguing in Publication Data
A catalogue record for this book is available from the British Library

Library of Congress Cataloging-in-Publication Data
A civilian occupation: the politics of Israeli architecture / edited by Rafi Segal, Eyal
Weizman; designed by David Tartakover... [et al.].
p. cm.
ISBN 1-85984-549-5
1. Architecture and state–Israel–History–20th century. 2. Architecture–Political
aspects–Israel. I. Segal, Rafi. II.Weizman, Eyal. III. Tartakover, David.

NA1477.C58 2003
720'.95694'09045-dc21

2003053507

Designed and typeset by Tartakover Design: David Tartakover and Onna Segev, Israel
Printed in the UK by The Cromwell Press, Trowbridge, Wiltshire.

TABLE OF CONTENTS

2   PHOTOGRAPHS / **MILUTIN LABUDOVIC**

15   PREFACE / **SHARON ROTBARD**

19   INTRODUCTION / **RAFI SEGAL, EYAL WEIZMAN**

28   SETTLEMENTS AND BORDERS / **ILAN POTASH**

32   SETTLEMENTS AS REFLEX ACTION / **OREN YIFTACHEL**

39   WALL AND TOWER / **SHARON ROTBARD**

59   THE PLAN / **ZVI EFRAT**

79   THE MOUNTAIN / **RAFI SEGAL, EYAL WEIZMAN**

100   THE BATTLE FOR THE HILLTOPS / **RAFI SEGAL, EYAL WEIZMAN**

108   MAP OF ISRAELI SETTLEMENTS IN THE WEST BANK,
      SETTLEMENT DATA / **B'TSELEM AND EYAL WEIZMAN**

120   PLANS OF SETTLEMENTS IN THE WEST BANK

144   PHOTOGRAPHS / **EFRAT SHVILY**

151   TO START A CITY FROM SCRATCH / **ERAN TAMIR-TAWIL**

162   AREA K / **NADAV HAREL**

167   THE LOWEST POINTS IN ISRAEL / **GIDEON LEVY**

174   BULLDOZER IN BETHLEHEM

176   PHOTOGRAPHS / **PAVEL WOLBERG**

184   IN THE LIGHT OF THE MORNING AFTER / **MERON BENVENISTI**

190   BIOGRAPHIES

Sharon Rotbard
PREFACE

E yal Weizman and Rafi Segal won an architectural competition
  organized by Israel Association of United Architects (IAUA), the
  representative body of Israeli architects, and were chosen to
prepare an exhibition of Israeli architecture at the Berlin Union
Internationale des Architectes (UIA) congress held in July 2002. Their
proposal, which included a plan for an exhibition and a catalog, aimed to
examine the role of Israeli architecture in the Middle East conflict.

The IAUA did not like this idea: a steering committee was
nominated, and, soon enough, the exhibition was cancelled under the
pretext of a low budget. After reading the catalog and examining David
Tartakover's graphic design, the same steering committee decided to
prevent its distribution, destroy the five thousand copies already printed
and withdraw support from Weizman and Segal's presentation.

This book is a second edition of the censored catalog, revised
by the editors and the contributors and re-designed by David Tartakover.

The debate on *A Civilian Occupation* and on its censoring has clearly
divided the Israeli architectural community between those who insist on
regarding architecture as a mere professional activity and those who do
not. But the flaring-up of the debate in itself, and its immediate spreading
from the local and architectural scenes to public and international arenas,
have also proven that architecture is not at all an innocent activity. On
the contrary, the debate has demonstrated that the work of Israeli
architects is at the very core of the political issues: there is nothing
innocent about regarding architecture as an autonomous process. Since
the shaping of the physical reality takes place on different scales, such as
the political, the urban and the architectural, architecture is no less
'political' than 'urban'. The very act of censoring the catalog was proof

that the denial of the political dimension of architecture is in itself a clear political statement. On the other hand, limiting the definition of architecture to only its 'architectural' dimension outlines an architectural doctrine according to which the role of architecture is to mask reality while creating it, to serve as a retreat from reality and as an alibi for escaping from it.

The questions posed by *A Civilian Occupation* extend this debate far beyond the contested frontiers of Israel and should be considered in a much broader context: How many architects would have declined the opportunity offered to architect Thomas Leitersdorf to design the city of his dreams? And how far would one go in investigating the true motives and real consequences of his commission? Is the architect really just an innocent professional or must he choose between obedient collaboration and militant action? And, finally, what is the role of politics within architecture and what is the role of architecture within politics? In these senses, the local debate initiated by Weizman and Segal should help generate new thinking on architecture, urbanism and politics. The politics of Israeli architecture is the politics of any architecture. It involves—to paraphrase some common architectural slogans—much more than 'more ethics and less esthetics': architecture is not just a magnificent game and urbanism is not always a gay science. To really appreciate them, you don't need to commit a murder. And if you can't be responsible, don't be irresponsible, because when more is more, enough is enough.

The private house of Israel's prime minister Ariel
Sharon in his Negev ranch is a living paradigm of
Israeli architecture: a mediterranean-style 'Wall
and Tower' with a new caravan outpost
photograph: Sharon Rotbard, 2002

Rafi Segal, Eyal Weizman
INTRODUCTION

N ational conflicts are characterized not only by rapid change and dramatic transformations. The slow process of building and the lengthy bureaucratic mechanisms of planning are as much a part of the scene on which territorial conflicts are played out.

Throughout the last century, a different kind of warfare has been radically altering the landscapes of Israel/Palestine. The mundane elements of planning and architecture have been conscripted as tactical tools in Israel's state strategy, which has sought to further national and geopolitical objectives in the organization of space and the redistribution of its population. The landscape has become the battlefield on which power and state control confront both subversive and direct resistance.

The relationship between the landscape and the Israeli-Palestinian conflict is symbiotic. The terrain dictates the nature, intensity and focal points of confrontation, while the conflict itself is manifested most clearly in the processes of transformation, adaptation, construction and obliteration of the landscape and the built environment.

In an environment where architecture and planning are systematically instrumentalized as the executive arms of the Israeli state, planning decisions do not often follow criteria of economic sustainability, ecology or efficiency of services, but are rather employed to serve strategic and political agendas. Space becomes the material embodiment of a matrix of forces, manifested across the landscape in the construction of roads, hilltop settlements, development towns and garden suburbs.

*

The exhibition *The Politics of Israeli Architecture* and its accompanying catalog *A Civilian Occupation* were intended to represent the Israel Association of United Architects (IAUA) at the Union Internationale des Architectes (UIA) Congress in Berlin in July 2002.

Both the exhibition and the catalog were conceived as an investigation of Israeli architecture by Israeli architects, scholars, photographers and journalists, and were meant to supplement the prevalent historical and political analysis of the conflict with a detailed description of its physical transformations. They were to be presented before an international gathering of architects and intended to highlight the fact that, because the Israeli-Palestinian conflict has a clear spatial dimension, architects and planners play an important, albeit little discussed, role in its unfolding. Architecture was presented as a political issue, and furthermore as the material product of politics itself.

The strategic use of territory in the exercise of state power is well established: state strategy is a profoundly spatial affair and as such reserves a primary role for the people who effect political goals with actual changes on the ground. But merely posing the question of the responsibility and culpability of Israeli architects and planners within the context of the conflict, and especially in the construction of the Jewish settlements in the West Bank, led to the exhibition being banned by the same body of architects that commissioned it, the IAUA.

Paradoxically, the very act of banning the exhibition had the direct effect of merging architecture and politics, and further established the architect as a political player. And, since architecture was thus accepted as an extension of politics, the questions remained: What politics? Whose politics? And what are its repercussions on the ground?

The essays in this book present the original material contained in the exhibition catalog for the first time since its banning. Occasional modifications have been made, and facts accumulated since its original intended publication have been incorporated.

The collection is composed of different 'episodes', each covering a particular chapter in the history of Israeli architecture and planning. Beginning in the pre-state days of Zionism, it moves through the period of early state planning and building to the colonization of the West Bank and Gaza by a series of Israeli governments.

Oren Yiftahel's article, 'Settlements as Reflex Action', first published in *Haaretz* in the summer of 2001, was the inspiration for the exhibition and opens the collection. It argues that deeply embedded within the Zionist DNA is the 'settlement instinct', the compulsive use of new settlements, within or outside Israel's international borders, for political reasons. It establishes an important link between the ethos of 'settling the land' and the use of planning for strategic and political purposes.

The essays following it are arranged chronologically: Sharon Rotbard demonstrates how the pre-state strategy of the paramilitary 'Wall and Tower' co-operative settlements made use of the double function of fortification and observation—a protective enclosure—that dominated their surroundings by the power of vision. These spatial technologies, upon which the political and military order of the frontier rested, became the mold in whose image all future Israeli urban planning was crafted.

Zvi Efrat's essay 'The Plan' deals with the early days of Israeli state planning. He demonstrates the extent to which Israel was turned into one of the planning laboratories of the modern era. In it, he argues, one of the most intense, comprehensive, controlled and efficient planning experiments was conducted. The article recounts the political, demographic and functional failures of this plan. Those failures lead to the next phase of Zionist planning experiments—the suburban sprawl into the areas occupied in the Six-Day War of 1967, and to our account of the history of the mountain settlements of the West Bank. Our essay underlines the evolution of the West Bank settlements from the early agricultural co-operatives to the right wing's religious suburbs. The text demonstrates how the landscape was appropriated into a system of domination and control, which is operated to a large degree by the civilian population.

Eran Tamir's interview with architect and town planner Thomas Leitersdorf, planner of Ma'ale Edummim and Emanuel in the West Bank, constitutes a first-hand account of the architect's role as the executive arm of political decisions. Leitersdorf is important in setting the benchmark for the design of mountaintop settlements in the West Bank. In a cool, analytical and professional tone, his interview is an insight into client-architect relations. It shows how deeply engraved within the praxis are political and strategic considerations, and how little they are acknowledged by the architect himself.

In his article 'The Lowest Points in Israel', Gideon Levy tells of the repercussions of settlements on Palestinian daily life. As a long-time human rights activist and columnist covering Palestinian human rights, his article attempts to describe the other pole on the axis of vision—the Palestinian view of the settlements from below. He describes the animosity of the Palestinians to the domestic monuments that have taken control of their land and freedom of movement.

Meron Benvenisti, a distinguished writer and columnist, former Deputy Mayor of Jerusalem and an expert on the Israeli-Palestinian conflict, wrote on 'the morning after'. His article, concluding this book, outlines two possible scenarios for the future of the settlements and the West Bank.

The photographs by Milutin Labudovic and Daniel Bauer are aerials taken as a part of Peace Now's[1] campaign to record the establishment and expansion of illegal outpost settlements in the West Bank. Beyond being mere recordings of settlement growth, they clearly show the contrast between the enclosed, pre-planned and sometimes pre-fabricated outpost settlements and the fabric of the Arab town.

The photographs by Nadav Harel, Efrat Shvily and Pavel Wolberg are critical portraits of building practices and daily life in the settlements taken at eye level. Nadav Harel's images are stills taken from his documentary *Area K*. In it, he traces the construction of a small fishing settlement on the northern shore of the Gaza Strip. Settlers talk to the camera in front of their newly built homes. The sense of an ideal and luxurious rural life is contrasted with the violence of its setting seen through the windows or over the fence.

The photographs by Efrat Shvily show settlements as ghost towns. Shot in 1993, they are a chilling testimony to the fact that so much of the construction on the West Bank is not market based but state directed, hence so many homes there remaining empty. This is true today. According to Peace Now, there are thousands of uninhabited dwellings in the West Bank. The civilian occupation relies on the presence of civilian architecture to demonstrate a Jewish presence across the landscape. In Shvily's photographs, architecture replaces human presence. The question of whether there are a pair of eyes looking out of the windows of settlement homes becomes irrelevant as the effect of domination is achieved by the mere presence of these buildings.

Pavel Wolberg is one of the most distinguished news photographers in Israel, covering especially military issues in the West Bank. His images describe settlement as a backdrop of activities, as sites of violence, domination and fear.

Historical photographs like the series by Zoltan Kluger accompanying Sharon Rotbard's 'Wall and Tower', and those collected by Zvi Efrat for his exhibition *The Israeli Project*, are taken with a different sentiment. They reflect to a large degree the bravado and euphoria prevalent in the creation of a new place and a new state, the self-conscious mise en scene of Zionism. But their presence alongside other critical images and texts makes their reading problematic.

The settlement master plans presented here for the first time, and the map of the West Bank, show how the occupation produced particular and locally developed spatial arrangements—the vernacular of occupation—whose function is discernible in their very form. These drawings are important components in the analysis of the relations between urban form and state power. By providing visual support to our article 'The Mountain', they demonstrate how directly and explicitly domination and control are inscribed into the way space is organized. The series of master plans, arranged according to the date of their construction and their topographical latitude, demonstrate a typological evolution in settlement form. The abstract layout of the co-operative agricultural settlements of the relatively flat Jordan Valley is replaced, with the change of power in Israeli politics, by the elastic and amorphous mountain settlements—rural suburbs, whose form attempts to adapt an ideal, concentric social and strategic model to diverse topographical conditions.

The map of the West Bank, researched and charted by Eyal Weizman for B'Tselem,[2] shows how the distribution of settlements across the landscape managed to generate the complete fragmentation of the terrain. The map marks precisely, and for the first time, the location, size and form of settlements and the enormous disparity between the area they cover, the boundaries of their jurisdiction, and the areas intended for their future growth. The success of the settlement project is made apparent in this drawing: how, with a built fabric comprising less than 2 per cent of the total land of the West Bank, settlements, strategically placed, managed to generate complete territorial control. What we see on the map as an end result was already clearly stated as an objective in early 1980s' masterplans.

Settlements constructed beyond the international border established in 1967 violate Article 49 of the Fourth Geneva Convention that states: 'The Occupying Power shall not deport or transfer parts of its own civilian population into the territory it occupies.' Settling Israeli citizens in the Occupied Territories thus contravenes international law.[3]

By taking up projects in the West Bank, Israeli architects cross yet another red line. Their planning conforms to a mode of design that serves to oppress and disrupt local populations. Thus, beyond the mere presence of Israeli settlements on occupied land, it is the way they were designed—their size, form and distribution across the terrain—that directly and negatively affects the lives and livelihoods of Palestinians. According to the regional plans of politicians, suburban homes, industrial zones, infrastructure and roads are designed and built with the self-proclaimed aim of bisecting, disturbing and squeezing out Palestinian communities. Israeli civilians are placed in positions where they can supervise vital national interests just like plain-clothes security personnel. This centralized, strategic and political use of planning was voluntarily transferred onto the ground by private architectural firms for financial gain. Planning and building in the West Bank is effectively executing a political agenda through spatial manipulations. The evidence is in the drawing.

It is by investigating the working methods and tools of architects—the lines drawn on plans, master plans, maps and aerial photographs—that the equation setting material organization against the abuse of power begins to unravel. Formal manipulations and programmatic organizations are the very stuff of architecture and planning, and it is in the very drawings that their effects are stated. In them, the forms produced by the processes and forces inherent within the logic of the occupation can be traced. In both its overall logic and the repetition of its micro-conditions, architecture and planning are used as territorial weapons. Settlement forms and locations are manipulated for the bisection of a Palestinian traffic artery, for surrounding a village, for supervision of a major city or a strategic crossroad. In the very act of design, the architect is engaged in the reversal of his professional practice. That is if, despite the banality and simplicity of the statement—and in the absence of an architectural equivalent of the medical profession's Hippocratic oath—planning and architecture must still be carried out to the benefit of society. That is if, the architect draws a particular angle, line or arc, or makes any other design decision that is explicitly and practically aimed at disturbance, suppression, aggression or racism, and when these stand, clearly and brutally, in breach of basic human rights, a crime has been committed.

Although, or perhaps because, settlements are not the efficient planning work of military engineers, but the result of architectural commissions by private architectural firms, the question of responsibility and liability must be addressed. Building matter, just like the tank, the gun and the bulldozer, is a weapon with which human rights are violated and crimes are being committed.

This statement opens up architecture to a different kind of critique. Beyond the mere reintroduction of morality and ethics into architectural debate, does this not also call for legal proceedings that should be prosecuted by international law?

Israeli architectural and planning practices differ in intensity (quantity) rather then in essence (quality) from other architectural practices around the world. Zionist history merged modern utopias with changing architectural and urban trends and grounded them in the context of a national-territorial conflict. In the history of Zionist urban and architectural form, each phase acted as a mirror image, distorted at times, of the style and methods of its time. But the conflict's violent intensity and its confinement to a limited space managed to accelerate the life span of urban and building types. Within and outside the West Bank, Israel can be seen as an example, an accelerator or even as a territorial laboratory playing alternative scenarios in fast-forward mode for the fate of these typologies.

Settlements are thus nothing but the final gesture in the urbanization of enclaves. Perfecting the politics of separation, seclusion and visual control, they can be seen as the end condition of contemporary urban and architectural formations such as enclaved suburban neighborhoods and gated communities. The ascent up the West Bank mountains coincided with the flight of the middle classes and their 'forting up' behind protective walls—both formations setting themselves against the poverty and violence of the Third Worlds they have produced. After all, is it not the same period of 1980s' Reaganism that has produced the greatest number of West Bank settlements and introduced the very terms 'gated community' and 'new urbanism'? Is the principle of exclusive bypass roads really that different from the deliberate carving up of poor communities with dead-end highways? Are we actually describing a unique place whose specificity renders its study a local curiosity, or is this not a worst-case scenario of capitalist globalization and its spatial fallout?

The Editors, Tel Aviv, November 2002

notes:

1. Shalom Achshav, Peace Now, the largest peace movement in Israel, has conducted 'Settlement Watch', a research project monitoring and documenting the building of new settlements and the expansion of existing ones since the Likud governments' massive building campaign in the Occupied Territories in the late 1980s. All aerial images in this book courtesy of Shalom Achshav. www.peacenow.org.il/English

2. B'Tselem—The Israeli Center for Human Rights in the Occupied Territories—endeavors to document and educate the Israeli public and policy-makers about human rights violations in the Occupied Territories, combat the phenomenon of denial prevalent among the Israeli public and help create a human rights culture in Israel. www.btselem.org

3. International humanitarian law relates to rules applying to states during times of war and occupation.
   The settlements in the Occupied Territories breach two primary instruments of international law: the Hague Convention on the Laws and Customs of War on Land, and its attached Regulations of 1907, and the Fourth Geneva Convention Relative to Civilian Persons in Time of War of 1949.

1.

Ilan Potash

SETTLEMENTS AND BORDERS

Israeli settlements

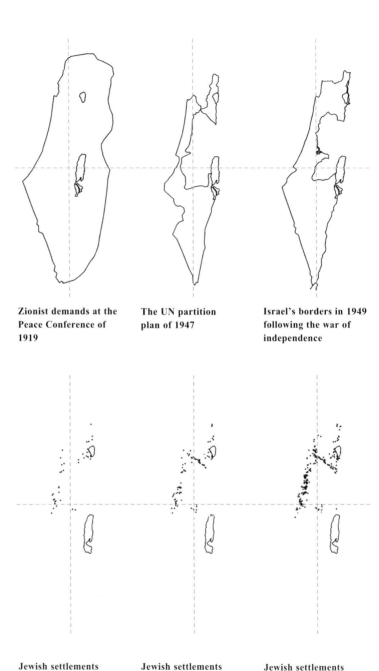

Zionist demands at the
Peace Conference of
1919

The UN partition
plan of 1947

Israel's borders in 1949
following the war of
independence

Jewish settlements
in 1914

Jewish settlements
in 1929

Jewish settlements
in 1939

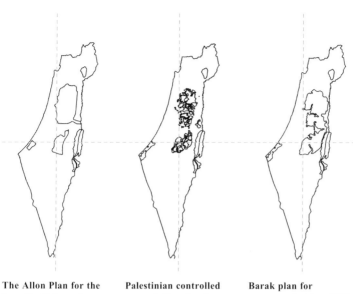

The Allon Plan for the
Israeli withdrawal
following the 1967 war

Palestinian controlled
areas A, B under the
Oslo Accords, 1993–1999

Barak plan for
permanent status, 2000

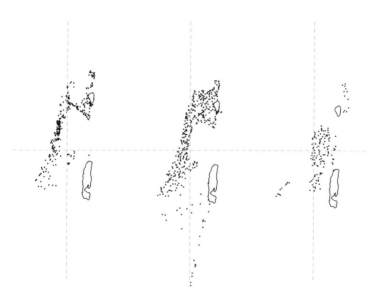

Jewish settlements
in 1948

Israeli settlements
within the 1967 borders

Jewish settlements in the
Occupied Territories, 2002

2.

Oren Yiftachel

SETTLEMENTS AS REFLEX ACTION

Q uite often, usually at times of crisis, and most commonly under the influence of Ariel Sharon, the Israeli government pulls a rabbit out of its hat—a settlement! In this vein we were told again last week about the impending establishment of five new Jewish settlements in the Halutza dunes, near the Gaza Strip.

Similarly, in June 2001 the Minister Responsible for State Lands, Avigdor Liberman, announced a plan for ten new Jewish suburban (or 'community') settlements along the Green Line,[1] north of Beer Sheva. Likewise, his colleague and Minister of Housing, Natan Sharansky, announced new housing plans for several West Bank settlements, most notably in Ma'ale Edummim, east of Jerusalem.

Like a reflex action, and without proper analysis, professional assessment or public debate, settlement decisions are taken almost daily in today's Israel. But these 'active' decisions, sadly and ironically, mark the paralysis gripping Israeli policy-making in recent years. Just as it was eighty, sixty, thirty, or ten years ago, new colonial activity is 'sold' as 'a proper Zionist response' to just about any challenge thrown up by the Palestinians or the Arab world. I have described this elsewhere as 'ethnocratic' politics, where the world is viewed through the lens of endemic ethnic conflict and a 'need' for constant expansion. 'Positive change' in the ethnocratic framework is only interpreted as a situation when *my* ethnic group grabs more resources and power from the *other*.

Given years of brainwashing, settlement activity is accepted by most, albeit not all, Israeli Jews as inevitable, something the nation truly needs. In the near future, then, the bulldozers will once again roll over the hills, flatten the earth, pave the land—and redemption will come to Zion! Why is all this problematic? Here are four main reasons.

First, new settlements damage Arab-Jewish relations.The obvious reason for the Halutza settlement plan is to block the possibility of this empty area being used in the future for territorial exchange with the Palestinians, in the framework of a peace agreement. The reader may remember that this was proposed at the Tabba summit as a possible step towards 'squaring the circle' that would allow Israel to annex several settlement blocs in the Occupied Territories, while still offering the Palestinians almost complete withdrawal.

This possibility still exists for future negotiations. Why should we block it deliberately and irresponsibly now? Why trample the remaining glimpse of a chance to reach an agreement and end the brutal and bloody occupation, and hence the disastrous al-Aqsa Intifada?

On a different level, the new settlement initiatives confirm once again the ongoing discrimination against the Bedouins in the south. For years the government has declared that the Bedouins must give up all their land claims and move into planned towns, because their settlements are 'too small' for the provision of modern services. Now the state is about to build new Jewish settlements far smaller than the Bedouin villages and they, needless to say, will receive full modern services from the outset.

The discrimination cries out—but nobody listens. What are the Bedouins supposed to think? Clearly, their alienation from the state will deepen, damaging Arab-Jewish relations even further.

Secondly, new settlements damage Israel's security. The link between national (Jewish) security and settlement has always been a cornerstone of the Zionist consensus, but this tie has never stood the test of conflict in real time since Israel gained its independence. Quite the contrary. In times of acute conflict, it was argued that the settlements would act as a security asset—on the contrary, they became a burden. This has been illustrated time and time again. For example, during the 1973 war, one of the principal emergencies involved the evacuation of Golan Heights settlements which engaged scarce combat units while risking the lives of soldiers. During the long conflict between Israel and Lebanon, too, near-border settlements became a major security headache, becoming easy targets for Hezbollah shelling. Most recently, the al-Aqsa Intifada has vividly shown that rather than enhancing Jewish security, the settlements in the West Bank and Gaza put large numbers of army and police personnel in real danger, while having no impact whatsoever on the porosity of the border to terrorists intending to act inside Israel.

The lesson is clear: a sovereign state should guard its territory with tanks, planes, army and border patrols. The argument that settlements enhance national security has mainly been a ploy to rally public support for ethnocratic and/or colonial expansion. This has little to do with the level of public security, or the safety of our communities and children. New settlements are a heavy security burden.

Thirdly, new settlements deepen social disparities. Due to the settlement mentality, embedded so deeply in the Israeli-Zionist psyche, Israel has already built over eight hundred Jewish settlements—the largest number of settlements per person in the world! As we know, most of the settlements on the periphery, especially in the Southern Negev and Northern Galilee, are economically weak and heavily dependent on government subsidies. These peripheral settlements—all built in the name of 'national goals', have often become loci of unemployment, alienation and poverty.

Now, instead of trying to buttress the hundreds of peripheral localities and improve the lives of their inhabitants by development and public investment, the government decides to build new ones. What is the likely effect? Many families from the older localities are likely to move into the newer, more attractive settlements. This means an emptying out of the most important asset these localities have: young mobile families.

This will no doubt have a draining effect on development towns, public housing estates or immigrant localities, whose communities are already desperately attempting to keep the young and the educated. The result, as proven over and over again, will mean an unnecessary increase in social gaps between center and periphery, and between the more affluent (and usually Ashkenazi—Jews of European descent) localities and their more deprived (usually Mizrahi—Jews of North African or Russian descent) counterparts.

Fourthly, new settlements generate a massive waste of public resources. The establishment of new settlements requires great investment, chiefly involving the construction of new infrastructures, including water, roads, electricity, education, health and housing. Given the high level of investment, it is no wonder that several state master plans, most notably 'Israel 2020' which was prepared during the 1990s by dozens of professional experts, recommended putting an end to the building of new settlements.

While making small concessions to the housing needs of culturally unique groups, such as Bedouins or ultra-Orthodox Jews, the plan argued strongly against the wastage involved in building new settlements. Other state development plans drawn up during the 1990s, such as National Plans 31 and 35, have made similar recommendations. What is the government's response? In defiance of the work of urban,

right: Allon, Jerusalem
region, Jordan Valley

photograph: Milutin Labudovic for
Peace Now, 2002

economic and social experts, it begins to construct new settlements.

One might ask: if the picture is so clear, why is settlement still going ahead? Beyond the powerful impact of the settling ethnocratic culture noted above, there are some influential groups that gain from the establishment of new settlements. Three such groups stand out. First, new settlers who usually come from the upwardly mobile groups who seek 'quality of life'. In Israeli society, this 'quality of life' is often a euphemism for the rush of middle-class families into gated, or controlled, suburban localities, 'protected' from the proximity of 'undesirables'. Second, the landholders, entrepreneurs and builders, who generally reap huge profits on the back of vast public investment. For them, this is a safe economic venture. The third group includes the cynical politicians who can wave the banner of 'activism' and 'initiative' during times of crisis, even though their activism is nothing short of disastrous. Our politicians are often bent on 'doing something', and quickly reach for one of the only things in which they have truly excelled—senselessly building new settlements.

These three groups work in quiet co-operation: they push the policy agenda, they all gain, and they remain silent on the cost to society at large. Israeli society must wake up and not let these small groups dictate its political and planning agenda. Riding on the coat-tails of empty and worn-out slogans such as 'national security', 'Zionist response', or 'building the frontier', these groups upgrade their own standing at the expense of the general public, and at the cost of sending Arab-Jewish relations into further disrepute.

There are indeed many good reasons to stand up and call out loud and clear, Stop! Don't waste millions from the public purse on yet another disastrous settlement venture, which lacks any logic, justice or foresight.

First published in Hebrew in *Haaretz*, 23 July 2001

note:

1. The Green Line was the ceasefire line between Israel and the Kingdom of Jordan from 1949 to 1967. See map p. 113.

3.

Sharon Rotbard

WALL AND TOWER (HOMA UMIGDAL)

THE MOLD OF ISRAELI ARCHITECTURE

M y second year of study at the Ecole Spéciale d'Architecture in Paris in 1987 was devoted to the study of vernacular architecture. Throughout the first semester we attended countless lectures on the influence of the climate on construction, the use of local materials, crafted building traditions, and even on something our teacher called 'critical regionalism'. Our assignment for term break was to raid our hometowns, dig up memories from ancestral homes, trace our roots back to obscure provincial villages, and rummage through old attics in search of old plans. My fellow students returned from their vacations loaded with precious loot: a cabin hidden in the Alps, a palace in the Shouf Mountains of Lebanon, a birdhouse in Provence, a Qasbah in Morocco, a cottage in Bergerac. I brought a model of *Homa Umigdal* (Wall and Tower) I had built out of popsicle sticks, just as I had built it some ten years earlier in the fourth grade. In my newly acquired French, I tried to present my somewhat convoluted point regarding 'the influence of a political climate on vernacular construction'. The teacher, who—according to rumors whispered in the hallways—had at one time been an active participant in the students' revolution of May 1968, looked at my haphazard model with wonder and asked, 'What is this Gulag?'

The most significant aspect of Israeli architecture, at once most evident yet so well concealed, is its political dimension. In Israel, architecture, just like war, is a continuation of politics through other means. Every act of architecture executed by Jews in Israel is in itself an act of Zionism, whether intentional or not. The political dimension of 'building the Land of Israel' is a fundamental, albeit often latent, component of every building in Israel, and the political realities it creates are often more dominant and conclusive than any stylistic, aesthetic, experiential or sensual impact they may have.

The official discourses of revival, settlement and construction of the new Jewish State have been the declared central ideas of Israeli architecture since its inception in the 1950s. The new place and a new construction were the site and the tool through which the project of settling the Jewish people in the Land of Israel was realized. They lay at the heart of the territorial conflict that followed, and became the central values and key metaphors of Israel's national ethos.

While acts of modern architecture were being formulated throughout the Western world under an illusion of their absolute autonomy, in Israel they were governed primarily by their political dimension. Within the complex relationship between architectural practice, architectural theory and political ideology that usually tends to exist, the political aspect dictated to the Israeli architect a new and paradoxical list of priorities, according to which political ideology and architectural theory merge, depend on each other, confront one another, yet are kept hidden one from the other. Israeli architecture has always been called upon to provide answers for the urgent needs of the time and, if possible, to proclaim itself as doing so. The architectural idea—the spirit of the built object and the added value of the act of building—serves at its best as a mere accessory, and at its worst as pure camouflage. The theoretical discourse of architecture has been pushed to the sidelines, becoming almost subversive while being transformed, in most cases, from the inspiration that imbues a building with meaning into an appendix, a superfluous addition that is used as a pretext, a justification, a cover-up.

Besides relinquishing the universal viewpoint held by Western architects, the defining essence of Israeli architecture is rooted between politics and architecture; this is where its dilemmas, its blind spots and its paradoxes are to be found. Israeli architecture produces impressive architectural objects but lacks a reflexive, comprehensive view of itself; it establishes facts cast in concrete that are inherently political, but it entirely lacks political awareness.

The nature of Israeli architecture's struggle for independence is primarily a national and territorial one, whose subject and object are the building of a sovereign state for the Jewish people. This is possibly the reason why we find so many variations of politically motivated construction in Israel: construction as a means of attaining territorial objectives, a means of deterrence, an educational tool, an official language, ideological rhetoric, or an industry for the fabrication of political realities.

Every practicing architect in Israel is confronted with a situation in which distinctive 'architectural' dilemmas are infused with critical political implications. Since its establishment, the State of Israel used the means provided by modern architecture to create its places. Both state and architecture were seeking a new place: the former needed one, and the latter strove to create one. Israeli architects at their best have always served the Zionist project to varying degrees of integrity, humility, dedication and responsibility, as they attempted to allow political ideology to infiltrate through architectural forms, and simultaneously enabled architectural doctrines to express themselves through programs inspired or even dictated by politics. In Israel, political ideology and architectural doctrine are interdependent and are in a constant and complex dialogue of justification and argumentation.

The *Homa Umigdal*[1] project, a system of settlement seemingly defensive but essentially of offensive form, was initiated in 1936 by the members of Kibbutz Tel Amal, today Kibbutz Nir David. The system was attributed to kibbutz member Shlomo Gur,[2] and was developed and encouraged by the architect Yohanan Ratner.[3] From the start, the objective of this communal and fortified type of settlement was to seize control of land that had been officially purchased by the Kakal (Keren Kayemet LeIsrael—known today as Israel's Lands Administration) but could not be settled. The system was based on the hasty construction of a wall made of pre-fabricated wooden molds filled with gravel and

surrounded by a barbed wire fence. All in all, the enclosed space formed a square-shaped area of 35m by 35m. Erected within this enclosure were a pre-fabricated wooden tower that commanded the surrounding area and four shacks that were to house a 'conquering troop' of forty people. Between 1936 and 1939, some fifty-seven such outposts were set up throughout the country, outposts which rapidly developed into permanent settlements of the kibbutz and moshav type.

The primary tactical requirement for the *Homa Umigdal* settlement was that it had to meet several conditions: it had to be planned in such a way that it could be constructed in one day, and later even in one night; it had to be able to protect itself for as long as it would take for backup to arrive; and it had to be situated within sight of other settlements and be accessible to motor vehicles.

The first *Homa Umigdal* outpost was erected at the site that later became Kibbutz Tel Amal in the Jezreel Valley. The members of the kibbutz had formed a community in Tel Aviv and were searching for land on which to settle. When several of them arrived at Kibbutz Beth Alpha, they realized that the members of that kibbutz wanted to establish another settlement east of their own, where there was a large Bedouin encampment, so that Beth Alpha would not be the most remote settlement.[4] The members of Kibbutz Tel Amal set up an encampment near Beth Alpha and began to cultivate the land. With the outbreak of the Arab Rebellion of April 1936, their attempts at settling the land were thwarted when the Bedouins set fire to their camp. These attacks led the people of Kibbutz Tel Amal to initiate lengthy discussions with the

Kibbutz Ein Gev members building a protective outer fence
photographs: Zoltan Kluger, 1937

residents of Beth Alpha and other settlements in the area regarding possible defense methods against the Bedouins, who were armed with 'shiny British rifles'. A formula was devised for the erection of four huts surrounded by sandbags. This promptly developed into double walls built as molds and filled in with gravel up to the height of the windows. 'In addition to that we aimed to erect observation posts in the corners,' wrote Yehezkel Frenkel, 'and near the huts to dig defensive fortifications.' The solution generated two objections: the first was that

this did not provide sufficient defense in the area in between the huts; the second, voiced by the carpenters, maintained that the walls would not withstand the pressure of the gravel. Following further calculations it became apparent that with little additional cost it might be possible 'to surround the huts with a yard and around the yard erect a wall and an observation tower with a light projector … [to] make a double mold and fill it with gravel'. Shlomo Gur went to consult Yohanan Ratner, and returned with 'a drafted plan of a rectangular wall with four defensive positions at its corners' (Frenkel). The proposal was transferred to the Regional Committee, which accepted the idea and declared that 'we are at the beginning of a new era of fortified walls, in spite of our neighbors' dismay.'

Following the success of the Tel Amal experiment, *Homa Umigdal* operations were carried out throughout the country. Tel Amal did not remain the furthest outpost for long—Kibbutz Sdeh Nahum was set up and within a year dozens of such outposts were set up throughout the country, 'sometimes seven outposts in a single night', recounts Gur, who participated in the organization of some fifty such operations. The nocturnal expeditions were always assisted by existing settlements in the area, and were co-ordinated by the Zionist leadership.

Homa Umigdal is the origin, the prototype, the model and the mold of Israeli architecture, as well as, to a large extent, the Israeli city. It is the metaphor of the Israeli practice of fait accompli. *Homa Umigdal* is the fundamental paradigm of all Jewish architecture in Israel, and it germinated the future characteristics of Israeli architecture and town planning: hasty translation of a political agenda into the act of construction, occupation of territory through settlement and infrastructure, high priority given to the buildings' security functions and military capabilities (both defensive and offensive), and informed use of modernity—organization, administration, prefabrication, logistics and communication.

Although as a metaphor the *Homa Umigdal* project holds a mythical status in the 'general history' of the State of Israel, and despite the active role this metaphor plays as a symbol of sacrifice, dedication and heroism in the civic education of every Israeli Jew, and its current incarnation in the tragic chronicles of our times, *Homa Umigdal* is blatantly absent from the canon of Israeli architecture, which has been busy over the past few decades fabricating a dubious narrative of the 'Tel Aviv Bauhaus' and with the selective historicization of the 'White City'. While putting all its efforts into canonizing the Israeli International Style, Israeli architecture has neglected not only one of the most architectonically unique elements of the 1930s, the only one that is entirely relevant to today's architecture, but also the sole element that received international acclaim in that decade. It is therefore hardly surprising that in 1937, one year after the establishment of Kibbutz Tel Amal, a model of *Homa Umigdal* was chosen for the Land of Israel Pavilion at the World Exposition in Paris—the one remembered in architectural history as the exposition that awarded the gold medal to Albert Speer's German pavilion. There are many similarities to be found between the idea of *Homa Umigdal* and the modern pavilion—a building type most familiar to us from international fairs and expos. The modernist canon is packed with pavilions and prototypes whose technology holds the potential of aggression, invasion and intrusion: the ready-made houses of 'Voisin', Le Corbusier's prototypes—the 'Citrohan' (1920–1922) that was meant to 'travel' to various types of landscape and the 'Cabanon' (1950) at Cap Martin, with which he was able to intrude into the life of Eileen Gray; the colonial residence machines of Jean Prouvé—the prefabricated, demountable 'Tropical House' (1949) and the 'House of the Lone Settler in the Sahara' (1957); the various prototypes of Buckminster Fuller's Dymaxion (1928–1945), his Geodesian Domes and, later, in the 1960s, their move from the hippie communes in California to the battlefields of Vietnam.

Like the pavilion, *Homa Umigdal* is characterized by its mobility (or potential mobility), careful logistical planning, prefabrication and the possibility of rapid construction and dismantling, and, most notably, by an assertive, dominant and spectacular presence. However, while the pavilion, as a 'rhetorical' building-type, a platform for ideas and manifestos, was a ceremonial expression of modern architecture's industrial utopia—a kind of allegory of prototypes—the *Homa Umigdal* project was a concrete implementation of it. *Homa Umigdal* is what happens when you let the pavilion escape from the architectonic zoo, when you allow the prototype to freely multiply itself: it turns into the ultimate machine of invasion.

Kibbutz Sde Nahum in the
Jezreel Valley / Kibbutz Hanita
in the Western Galilee

Homa Umigdal almost allegorically expresses the characteristics and dilemmas of the Israeli built environment, revealing the tensions between its simultaneous impulses and internal contradictions. It is the site of all the Israeli oxymorons—'offense through defense', 'intrusive siege', 'the camp as a home', 'introverted expansion', 'permanent temporality', 'house-arrest'. The figure of the oxymoron is carved deep into the genetic code of the Zionist Enterprise itself and has accompanied it since Theodor Herzl wrote his novel Altneuland ('The Old New Land') and since the concrete translation of his vision into the city of Tel Aviv.[5] The figure of the oxymoron stands at the root of the concept of Israel as a 'democratic Jewish state'.

Homa Umigdal is more an instrument than a place. It is a rough draft of a place, an almost dimensionless point in space: an observation point, an all-seeing eye that cannot see itself. As a strategy, *Homa Umigdal* realized the impulse for expansion through territorial conquests by establishing new 'settlement points', a term that in itself hints at the fact that the 'point' on the map was more important than the 'settlement' itself. The location of the settlement as part of a greater strategic plan was

of greater importance than its actual existence, and the location was determined according to optimal vantage points: the *Homa Umigdal* network was spread out in such a way that every outpost had eye contact with another, enabling the towers to transmit messages by Morse code using flashlights at night and mirrors during the day.

In total contrast to its ambitions of expansion, the tactical and strategic solution offered by *Homa Umigdal* served in fact to perpetuate the ghetto mentality and the impulse of enclosure. The priorities of the

Homa Umigdal outposts stipulated that the wall was to be built first, then the observation point and, only at the end, the houses themselves. Much has been said and written about the link between external threats to the State of Israel, whether real or imagined, and the formation of social unity and national cohesion (especially these days, when the war with the Palestinians has not only brought upon us a National Unity Government, but has also blurred social tensions and stunted the sectoral politics that sprang up during the last decade in Israel, in the days of the 'New Middle East' and the peace process). In *Homa Umigdal*, we are shown exactly how this link is established: the seclusion within the wall separates the settlement from its new environment and defines the new community not only as those who choose to live 'inside', but as those who are under potential threat from outside.

Shlomo Gur himself admitted that one of the reasons that Tel Amal searched for land on which to settle was in order to prevent the dismantling of the kibbutz. This same principle holds true on a global scale as well, since the State of Israel's self-definition depends on the fact that it was established first and foremost as a shelter for Jews

Tel Amal, Beth Shean Valley / Members of the Special Night Squad driving into Kibbutz Maoz Haim
photographs: Zoltan Kluger, 1937

threatened with extermination by the Nazi regime. The organization of Israel's land is also based on this principle, as the degree of communal unity is directly connected to the imminence and intensity of external threats. The cross between hasty settlement through military or para-military means in civilian camouflage, seclusion behind fortifications and an ideologically homogenous community has repeated itself countless times since the days of *Homa Umigdal*. The 'settlement point' system has been implemented in national master plans throughout

Israel's history, such as the plan drawn up in the 1970s for Judaizing the Galilee, and the current uninstitutionalized expansion of settlements in the Occupied Territories. In all these cases, a large degree of ideological and social homogeneity was retained—whether through an existing core of founders, or through mechanisms that filter new residents according to social or economic criteria. Whatever the reasons for this homogeneity—security, ideological or economic—the repetition of this settlement pattern, in which there is a distinct congruence between geographic area and social status, ideology or ethnic identity, has been one of the most prominent characteristics of the built Israeli landscape.

'The camp is your home, guard it well.' This slogan, posted in countless military bases, can be seen as the essence of the settlement program. If the camp is our home, and if it must be guarded, the fate of the camp's residents is to become prisoners of their own gaze. The constant panoptic observation policed by the vantage point of the 'tower'[6] determined the overpowering relations between the *Homa Umigdal* settlements and their surroundings even before the actual cultivation of the land and its economic exploitation through agriculture or development. In *Homa Umigdal*, the settlement point on the map is indeed a point within a strategic network of points, but on the ground it is first and foremost an observation point.

Henri Lefebvre characterized agrarian time and space as a heterogeneous combination of variables such as climate, fauna and flora, while claiming that the industrialized time and space tends towards homogeneity and unity.[7] As an initiative whose intention was to organize the logistics of the gaze, *Homa Umigdal* transformed, literally from one day to the next, the territory which it occupied. Despite the fact that the landscapes where the outposts were located have always been agrarian frontiers, this organized observation point was sufficient to transform the territory into an industrialized space. Only a few such panoptic observation points had the power to unify an entire agrarian landscape—to eradicate, through the strategic threat, the complex economic and cultural differences that distinguished between the Arab Bedouins, farmers and urban population. *Homa Umigdal* was the spearhead of industrialization, not only because of its logistical and technological characteristics, but also because it transformed the entire environment into an object under the scrutiny of industrial and instrumental observation. This vantage point had its own accompanying technologies such as the tower, the binoculars and the light projector, and was organized as a systematic project that had to be managed and manned. Beyond the military implications of this vantage point, in terms of Paul Virilio's 'I see, therefore I kill',[8] the very instrumentalization of the territory through the gaze invests the landscape with scenarios and schemes, threats and dangers, infuses places and objects with tactical possibilities, situates them within a strategy and unifies them into one 'political' space.[9] It transforms the landscape into a battlefield, a scene of conflicts, a frontier—in fact, into a city.

In *Homa Umigdal*, the image is one of 'work in progress', a permanent construction site, a production line. The hyperactivism of transformation and construction was in absolute contrast to the passivity of the land. The Land of Israel was a virgin land to be possessed. The Land of Israel was perceived as a clean slate, a tabula rasa, as raw material awaiting the sculptor. This perception lived on in the State of Israel, which became a place of perpetual motion from the temporary to the permanent and back again, a place whose core essence was not its permanency, but that of movement and change. If one day the 'right of return' is granted to the Palestinians, it is very doubtful whether the returning refugees will find their way home—that is, if it still exists.

Contrary to the illusions of permanency with which we are usually provided by urban and pastoral landscapes, and contrary to the static impression left by historic settlement patterns, the new Israeli settlement pattern has always been perceived as a dynamic process, focused on its power to transform rather than on becoming a permanent reality. Modern Zionism was infused with the inspiration of the industrial and colonial initiatives of the nineteenth century. If compared with Herzl's vision of 'The Canal of the Seas'—the construction of a man-made canal which was meant to replace and eventually close off the Suez Canal—*Homa Umigdal* was a humble act of industrialization of the environment, with the large-scale operations coming later. The State of Israel initiated immense transformations in the geography of the country: seas were dried up, roads were laid, a network of infrastructure was spread out, ports were excavated, forests were planted, deserts were made to bloom, towns and cities were founded. In Israel, every view of the landscape is merely a single frame taken from one continuous documentary film. Every photograph is only a coincidental image in an endless saga. In the same way, every built object is perceived according to its circumstances; always as a single co-ordinate on the long path of construction or ruin.

The efforts of settlement involved a series of tasks, some of which were military and tactical, others civilian and strategic. This dualism was expressed in slogans such as 'One hand on the plough, the other on the sword.' Despite the military means often used, a civilian appearance has always been, and still is, one of the Zionist Enterprise's most important strategic objectives. This is the reason why *Homa Umigdal* and the later mechanisms of settlement left the status of the place and the residents themselves in doubt. In every type of politically-motivated settlement enterprise in the country, whether or not backed by the establishment, there exists a paradoxical mixture of a civilian and a military operation: a military operation camouflaged in civilian clothes, civilians recruited under the patronage of the army.

'Civilianization' is the transformation of the soldier into the pioneer—who is able, if need be, to change his clothes and transform back into a soldier at any time—and the transformation of the camp into a home is the description also assigned to the transformation of the paramilitary outpost into a permanent settlement. This is the reason why the apparent preservation of normality, of routine civilian life, has always had to be backed by military and tactical operations, which in the long run demand far greater funds than the act of settlement itself: in Israel, the mundane is a strategic weapon.

As time went by and new settlements were founded using more sophisticated means, the two essential functions of *Homa Umigdal*—fortification and observation—held fast and repeated themselves on every scale. They dictated the location of the new settlements on mountain peaks and hilltops. They molded the entire landscape as a network of points, as an autonomous layer spread above the existing landscape, transforming the country by dividing it, not according to natural, territorial divisions, but according to dromological[10] divisions, according to the speed of transportation and the lines of infrastructure. Thus in the Occupied Territories today we find two countries superimposed one on the other: on top, 'Judea and Samaria', the land of settlements and military outposts, bypass roads and tunnels;

and underneath, 'Palestine', the land of villages and towns, dirt roads and paths. Ultimately, the essence of *Homa Umigdal* had a decisive influence on the way Israelis perceive the space in which they live, which in turn maps out the values themselves: the observers versus the observed, a Cartesian ghetto versus a chaotic periphery, a threatened culture versus 'desert makers' (in the words of Ben-Gurion), city versus desert, future and past versus present, Jews versus Arabs.

Homa Umigdal initiated an original tradition of local Trojan horses, machines of infiltration and other types of ambulatory, temporary, political and hyperactive objects: the tent in the outpost and the mobile home in the settlements. These banal objects are ostentatious not because of the way they look, but rather because of the outward display of their potential for mobility, expansion and transformation; because they threaten to transform the temporary into the quotidian, the quotidian into the permanent and the permanent into the eternal; because of the way they represent all these possibilities in the landscape in order to transform the land itself into an arena of struggle and power.

Shlomo Gur saw in his invention only a prosaic answer to the problems of the new settlement: he always claimed to be indifferent to their visual effectiveness. The type of interpretation made here would be entirely alien not only to the axiomatic perception he had of his system, but also to his character as a 'man of action'. But Gur himself was always accompanied by the photographer Zoltan Kluger to the new *Homa Umigdal* settlements. It is also hard to ignore the fact that the settlements of Ein Gev, Massada and Sha'ar Hagolan were the subject and the location of the first Hebrew technicolor film ever shot in Israel, *Spring at Galilee*, by Efraim Lisch (13 minutes, 1939), and that the settlement of Hanita was celebrated in the first Hebrew opera *Dan the Guard*. The opera was based on Sh. Shalom's play *Shootings at the Kibbutz* (1936) and was adapted in 1939 by the composer Marc Lavry and the newly immigrant writer Max Brod (!). The opera was performed on thirty-three evenings in Tel Aviv in 1945. In any case, it's hard to ignore the simple fact that even without Kluger's photographic documentation, the mere appearance of new settlements was a spectacular event, an act of creating something from nothing, a spectacle of light[11]—the nocturnal and daylight signaling, and sometimes even the trajectories of tracer bullets and the echoes of explosions.

However, as is usually the case in Israeli architecture, the actual object is much more powerful than any image or metaphor. The real spectacularity of *Homa Umigdal* did not stem from the way it looked but from what it was, from what it did. Beyond the fact that the wall was a program, and was destined to become an 'ideology', it was, first and foremost, a *wall*; it was a plain wooden mold of 20 centimeters width filled with gravel. The wall was a premonition of things to come, because whoever is able to fill the mold with gravel will not hesitate to fill it with other materials. Beyond the fact that it was an ad hoc protective wall, whose job it was to prevent infiltration of unwanted visitors and to provide protection from bullets, the wall was a technological presentation and a logistic tour de force: it was the promise, the non-explicit threat of concrete.

notes:

1. The accounts of settlements and the quotations are taken from a conversation between Shlomo Gur and Ariella Azoulay, the main points of which were revealed in Azoulay's book, *How does it look to you?*, Tel Aviv: Babel, 2000, pp.27–35; *10 Years*, a Tel Amal booklet, 1946, p. 30; Yehezkel Frenkel, 'How we arrived at *Homa Umigdal*', in *40 years of Homa Umigdal*, a Tel Amal booklet, p. 21; Shlomo Gur, the man behind *Homa Umigdal* (a monologue recorded by Ze'ev Aner in The Days of *Homa Umigdal*), editor: Mordechai Naor, Idan Series, Jerusalem: Yad Ben-Zvi Press, 1986, pp. 47–50.

2. Shlomo Gur (Gerzovsky) (1913–2000) was a founding member of Kibbutz Tel Amal and became a sort of national 'project manager' following his success as the founder of *Homa Umigdal*. Before the establishment of the state, he was responsible for planning the defense constructions of many settlements including those of the Old City of Jerusalem. Following the establishment of the State of Israel, he was charged with the country's first *grands projets*: the Hebrew University, the National Library and the Knesset building in Jerusalem.

3. Yohanan Ratner (1891–1965), a trained architect and a former Red Army officer, was the chief architect and strategic planner of the Hagana, the pre-state precursor of the Israel Defense Forces (IDF). He later became a

general in the IDF. As a member of the central
command during the War of Independence, Ratner was
the only general who received Ben-Gurion's
permission to retain his non-Hebrew surname. Later he
served as Dean of the Faculty of Architecture at the
Haifa Technion. As a teacher and dean in the 1950s,
Ratner was considered a reactionary and one of the
more ardent opposers of modernist architecture.

4. Although the land surrounding Kibbutz Beth Alpha had
been bought by the Jewish National Fund (JNF) from
Arab landowners in Beirut, it was being used by the
Bedouins as pasture every winter and could not be
settled upon.

5. *Altneuland* was published in 1902. In this futuristic novel,
inspired by the tales of Jules Verne, Herzl follows the
adventures of a young Jewish intellectual from Vienna,
Dr. Friedrich Lowenberg, who meets a mysterious
character by the name of Kingscourt. Lowenberg and his
companion decide to dissociate themselves from the
decadent European lifestyle, and settle on a desert island
in the Pacific Ocean. On their way, they pass through the
Land of Israel and find it in a state similar to the one
Herzl found during his historic visit to Palestine in 1898.
After ten years on the island, Lowenberg and Kingscourt
decide to resume their travels. They return to the Land
of Israel and discover *Altneuland*—the old-new land
that had been built and settled according to Herzl's
program in his book, *The Jewish State*. The first
translation of *Altneuland* was edited by Nachum Sokolov
and was published in 1904 under the biblical title *Tel
Aviv*, borrowed from the *Book of Ezekiel*. This is what
perhaps made Tel Aviv, which was founded five years
later in 1909, into the only city in the world to be named
after a book.

6. See Roland Barthes' renowned text *The Eiffel Tower* and
Michel Foucault's *Surveiller et Punir* for more
on the way observation from a tower 'intellectualizes' a
landscape. Ariella Azoulay links this birds-eye view to
another of Shlomo Gur's projects: in 1937, Gur took a
series of photographs of the roofs of Jerusalem's Old
City, in order to plan the defense of the Jewish Quarter.
Azoulay, who gives a detailed description of these
photographs in the introduction to her published
conversations with Gur, interpreted them as a model of
'the official eye of the State of Israel' (Azoulay, *How
does it look to you?*, p. 28). The mythological slogan
spontaneously invented by a tired IDF soldier a moment
after the successful assault on Mount Hermon in 1973,

who called it 'the eyes of the state', should also be noted in this context.

7. Henri Lefebvre, 'Espace et Politique', in Henri Lefebvre, *Le Droit à la Ville*, Paris: Éditions Anthropos, 1968, p. 207.
8. In this context, one cannot ignore the work of my teacher, Paul Virilio, especially his book *War and Cinema*, London and New York: Verso, 1999.
9. This is a concrete example of Lefebvre's claim that 'landscape that has undergone instrumentalization becomes a political landscape', Lefebvre, 'Espace et Politique', pp. 277–8.
10. In Virilio's terms.
11. See for example Paul Virilio's explanation of the link between the searchlights of anti-aircraft batteries during World War II and the emblem of 20th Century Fox, as well as other spectacular expressions such as Albert Speer's Cathedral of Light in Nurnberg.

right: **Volunteers helping to establish Kibbutz Ein Gev in the Galilee**
photograph: **Zoltan Kluger, 1937**

4.

Zvi Efrat

THE PLAN
DRAFTING THE ISRAELI NATIONAL SPACE

'Everything will be systematically worked out in advance. In the elaboration of this plan, which I am capable only of suggesting, our keenest minds will participate. Every achievement in the fields of social science and technology of our own age and of the even more advanced age, which will dawn over the protracted execution of the plan, must be utilized for the cause. Every happy invention that is already available or will become available must be used. Thus the land can be occupied and the State founded in a manner as yet unknown to history, with unprecedented chances of success.'

Theodor Herzl, *Der Judenstaat* (*The Jewish State*), 1896[1]

'The great revolution is not over yet, and its essential functions have barely begun. In the near future we must lay foundations that will stand for decades and possibly centuries to come. We must shape the character of the State of Israel and prepare it to fulfill its historical mission.'

David Ben-Gurion, *The War Diary*, January 1949[2]

As it is—crowded, heaped up and frantic at the center, diffused, dissociated and monotonous at the margins—the fabricated space of Israel is a 'manner of land occupation and state founding without an historical precedent'. Contrary to common belief and visual impression, it was born not of haphazard improvisation, emergency solutions or speculative entrepreneurship, and certainly not of spontaneous diachronic development, but rather of the unprecedented objective of putting into practice one of the most comprehensive, controlled and efficient architectural experiments of the modern era.

Indeed, this is Israel's singularity among nation-states. It was 'systematically worked out in advance', formulated a priori by means of arithmetical, planimetrical and demographic formulas, drafted in pencil, ink and watercolor by planning professionals from various disciplines, who were called upon to actualize Ben-Gurion's prescript 'to transform the country, the nation, our entire modes of life'; or, to put it in more technical terms, to engineer and re-design (no less) the country's geographic, ecological and agronomic mold—its patterns of urbanization, socialization and employment, the overall framework of production and service, the character of its public life as well as its patterns of domestication in the new Israeli state. An all-embracing planning ambition such as this is not self-evident even in the context of its own period—one that revered the 'planning sciences' and perceived mega-architects, infra-engineers, macro-economists and sociology-masters as the omnipotent agents of progress itself.

Precedents for the Israeli project can be found in Stalin's Five-Year Plan for the Soviet Union, in the American New Deal infrastructural projects and public works of the 1930s, in the German National-Socialist regional plans for the occupied territories of Poland and in the post-World War II British schemes of New Towns. However, its sweeping vision, exceeding all instrumental models and circumstantial explanations, is rooted in the utopian imagination and the topian (to use Martin Buber's neologism) praxis of the Zionist movement. These roots call for some elaboration, so as to re-enact the bedding upon which the 'master plan' of Israel was drafted immediately upon the 'outbreak' of the state.

The very notion of 'Hamifal Hazioni' (the Zionist Enterprise or Zionist Project) enfolds the highly institutionalized, explicitly synthetic and actively constructive nature of the process of land appropriation (or re-appropriation) and nation-building by the Jews in the twentieth century. Any attempt to 'normalize' Zionism by over-emphasizing aspects such as spontaneous immigration, organic settlement or market forces misses the point: the artificial essence of Zionism, the grounding of its rhetoric in the notion of 'negation', 'inversion', 'synthesis' or 'combination'; its self-definition as a constrained, corrective, redemptive (Ben-Gurion even used the notion of 'messianic') intervention in historical time and geographic space. In this context, centralized planning is the ultimate trope that binds Words and Things; it is the Zionist spirit itself, emanating from layers of fictional prose, ideological manifestos or programmatic protocols and printed on the landscape over and over again with every new spatial move or architectural object.

The most conspicuous use of centralized planning—not merely for territorial organization, but rather as an apparatus molding a new ethos—is manifested in the consistent efforts to shift the political, cultural and economic weight from the city to the countryside and from

the center to the periphery. As a rule it may be said that, in its first fifty years, the Zionist movement devised and developed a range of pioneering models of agricultural settlement supported by sophisticated logistics of manufacture, organization and marketing, but never imagined, planned or actually built a city. In fact, the modern metropolitan city was consistently portrayed in both literary utopias and direct propaganda as anathema to the Zionist concept of land redemption—a parasitic growth threatening to undermine the fundamental values of the re-emerging Hebrew civilization.

Thus, revolutionary objectives, totally controlled planning and a well-co-ordinated course of action characterized the Zionist Enterprise from its very outset. However, the country's crucial 'conversion' was obtained with the founding of a sovereign state. The end of the British

Mandate in 1947 and the ensuing administrative vacancy, the war of 1948 and the ruinous grounds created, the exchange of refugee populations during the war and immediately following it, the confiscation and nationalization of over 90 per cent of the country's lands, the emergency legislation (most of which is still in force today) and the austerity decrees, the virtually absolute monopoly of Mapai (Israel Labor Party) over all state and Histadrut (Federation of Labor Unions in Israel) apparatuses, the moral and material support provided by the world's superpowers for the new state (specifically, the budget allotted for development, which was separate and equal in size to the comprehensive national budget)—all came together to provide an opportunity and ostensible legitimization for a project of construction (and obliteration) more daring than any of its imagined precedents.

Only a few weeks after the Declaration of Independence, during the war of 1948 and as a means of pushing forth its goals, Arieh Sharon, a Bauhaus graduate and one of the prominent architects of Israel's Labor Movement, was commissioned to establish the governmental Planning Department.[3] Within about a year, this department presented an overall master plan for Israel (known as the Sharon Plan) and provided the political leadership of the time with a powerful tool for molding a new landscape and dictating the shape of things to come. Professionally speaking, the Sharon Master Plan is by no means an innovative document. Rather than original ideas, it presents an assemblage of models, theories and experiments, some of which had been developed locally during the British Mandate era, mainly by members of the Settlement Reform Forum; others were imported from Europe as ready-mades and abruptly naturalized. In fact, the Plan is unique only in its scope—in its ambition to put forth at once a single layout, a single vision, a single stately concept at a scale of 1:20,000. Such ambition could have remained anecdotal—too rational, instrumental and progressive or alternatively, too dreamy, ritualistic and reactionary—had it not been implemented verbatim, almost entirely, often by short-cutting standard planning procedures; always through the systematic reproduction of zoning doctrines, building typologies and construction methods.

While it had no statutory status (or perhaps precisely because it did not have to face legislation procedures),[4] the Sharon Plan transformed within less than a decade a document of principles into a mega-project embracing dozens of cities and towns and hundreds of rural settlements ex machina; extensive woodlands, national parks and nature resorts ex fabrica; networks of roads, electricity, water, ports and factories ex nihilo. Soon after the official publication of the Plan in 1950, Sharon and his team of planners realized that they had provided the government with an all too readable building manual. In spite of their enduring commitment to overall centralized planning and their loyalty to the party, they made efforts to slow down the literal application of their plan on the ground. However, the genetic code they had devised on paper in their laboratory had already been cloned and disseminated throughout the country, proving its durability in vivo, even under the most adverse conditions.[5]

The pressing national task assigned to Sharon and his team of planners was providing temporary housing solutions for the masses of new Jewish immigrants and settling the country's borderlands in order to stabilize the 1948 cease-fire lines, prevent territorial concessions and inhibit the return of Palestinian war refugees. The planners accomplished this by drafting a statewide network of civil frontiers composed of transit camps and agrarian outpost settlements, as well as by re-settling deserted Arab villages with new Jewish immigrants (mainly those from Asia and North Africa). Concurrently, a long-term mission was outlined: preparing a plan for 'the country's intense and comprehensive development, which would reach all its corners'.

Just one year after its processing began, the first draft of the Sharon Plan was presented. Its objectives were targeted towards a local population of 2,650,000 inhabitants (a target obtained in 1966), which would be dispersed throughout the country, thus adjusting the 'anomaly', or the 'colonialist pattern', as the planners dubbed the development of the Jewish community in the country during the British Mandate. Upon the establishment of the State of Israel, two thirds of the Jewish population was concentrated in the three large cities: Tel Aviv, Jerusalem and Haifa. Eighty-two per cent lived along the coastal plain. The aim of the Sharon Plan was that only 45 per cent of the urban population would dwell in the big cities, while 55 per cent would settle in the new medium-sized and small towns.

De-territorialization (effective upon the local Palestinian population but by and large futile vis-à-vis the veteran Jewish population) and de-centralization (according to the strategic precept of using civilian settlements as military outposts de jure or de facto, a precept developed in the early pre-state days and valid to this day) formed a consecrated cause, which dictated all moves and procedures of the national plan, even if at times they were inconsistent with professional discretion, even if they entirely failed the test of economic logic, and even if they turned the 'melting-pot' rhetoric against itself and created, in effect, severe geographic and social segregation between veteran residents and new immigrants. Mass immigration was both the problem and the solution. The problem: the immigrants' predispositions regarding the choice of their place of residence were known in advance and considered by the authorities a threat to the Zionist settlement policy.

Prefabricated tin homes and public housing in the
Yokne'am Immigrant Transit Camp
photographer unknown, 1951

66

Thorough studies of the colonization patterns in New World countries carried out by the planning committee indicated that in Israel too, without decisive state intervention, the first generation of immigrants would undoubtedly choose to crowd the coastal cities, thereby deepening the Mandatory 'anomaly' even further and accentuating the emptiness of the rural regions. The solution: were it not for the statistical body of new immigrants, the historical opportunity to re-invent the Israeli space would not have emerged. Indeed, in spite of the considerable propagandist endeavors invested by the government in the attempt to induce a population migration to the periphery, it was clear to leaders and planners alike that the Sharon Plan would not be voluntarily implementable.

Eliezer Brutzkus, one of the senior conceivers of the Plan, described its achievements post factum vis-à-vis the relevant model— namely, the construction enterprise of the new workers' towns in the Stalinist Soviet Union: 'Truth be told, these results were obtained here too, against the free will of the settled subjects, namely the immigrants, through a method whose underlying principle was "straight off the boat to development regions". We must not forget the basic fact that the creation of the New Towns, and the settlement of the peripheral regions, were done primarily through directing the new immigrants, and only marginally by attracting the "veteran population."'[6]

The Soviet project, efficient as it was in constructing and inhabiting, top-down, hundreds of new provincial towns and edge cities, was not the only model from which the Israeli planners drew inspiration.[7] The rehabilitation projects of Western Europe after World War II, especially the new satellite towns around London founded by the British Labour government, were also thoroughly analyzed by Sharon and his team (the planner Sir Patrick Abercrombie, the 'father of the New Towns', was even invited to Israel and met with Ben-Gurion). In the Israeli laboratory—and this is the enigma of its proletarian charm—a new paradigm was created, based on the unlikely marriage of a suburban garden city in a Western welfare state and a peripheral industrial town on the outskirts of the Bolshevik Empire. This juxtaposition embodies the two formative paradoxes ingrained in the Sharon Plan: the attempt to concoct, synchronize and monitor a rational mechanism for 'organic', 'regionalist' and quasi-historical settlement; and the unequivocal ideology of anti-urban urbanization (as many towns and as little urbanism as possible).

The basic tool suggested by the Plan for achieving this original construct was the re-division of the country into twenty-four districts, designed mathematically to contain an equal number of residents. The districts were determined according to geographic characteristics and were planned as arrays of agricultural settlements clustered around central villages and served by a regional town. Size, dimension and amount (of population, area, employment) were perceived as reliable criteria for obtaining the desired interactions between center and periphery, city and country, industry and agriculture.

Over four hundred agrarian settlements were founded during the state's first decade according to the Plan's guidelines, but its epitome was the creation of the district town—the infamous Development Town—whose optimal size was the subject of lengthy academic discussion among the planners. Ultimately, the preferred model was of an intimate town, housing between twenty thousand and fifty thousand residents, assumed to be exempt from the disorientation, alienation, social injustice, speculative realty and other urban malaises associated with the cosmopolitan city. (Was it also a return, mutatis mutandis, of the repressed *shtetl* still haunting the planners?)

In order to prevent the development of unruly colonization and socialization patterns typical of New World countries at all costs, the Sharon Plan chose to emulate the European historic layout, whereby the majority of the population dwells in small and medium-sized towns integrated into the agricultural hinterland, and only the minority lives in the big cities. The origins of this hierarchic web lie in pre-industrial agrarian culture, and reflect centuries of moderate organic growth. The planners of Israel tried to squeeze this process into a single heroic decade, backing their ambitions with intricate pseudo-scientific theories that analyzed the link between settlement patterns and endurance during times of crisis. (An especially authoritative model for the Israeli planners was the 'Theory of Central Places', formulated by German geographer Walter Christaller through his 1939 doctoral research.[8])

Such a general attitude of activating a regressive revolution, or a pioneering Old World, may be discerned not only in the dispersal of towns and settlements on the map, but also in the attempt to base the

Kisalon, the first moshav olim (agrarian settlement
for new immigrants) in Israel, Jerusalem Corridor
photographer unknown, 1950

architecture of the towns themselves on a conceptual crossbreeding between mechanistic planning methods striving to render the traditional city more efficient in terms of mass housing and motor vehicle traffic on the one hand, and more picturesque conceptions on the other, willed to tone down the city by deconstructing it into small, autonomous communities, protected from street life, zoned off from industrial sectors and wrapped in green pastoral surroundings. The planners believed that through critical study of urban history they had managed to develop an innovative method for ideal city planning, as can be gathered from the writings of Eliezer Brutzkus: 'The structure of the New Towns is determined by their division into Neighboring Units. This method differs from conservative methods of urban planning still prevalent in the old cities in Europe as well as in Israel. These cities are built as a monotonous continuum of houses, streets and residential neighborhoods, dragging on endlessly and making the lives of their residents gray and dull.' (The author goes on to explain the conceptual superiority of cities such as Ofakim, Kiryat Shmona or Ashdod, over Paris, Berlin, or Vienna.)[9]

The neighboring units mentioned above (or 'eggs' as they were called in the professional milieu) are the structural organizing principle of the New Towns. In theory, they were intimate urban sections with biomorphic contours that rejected orthogonal grids and endowed the 'instant' towns with elasticity and vibrancy. In reality, the separation into autonomous units created a jumbled grouping of disembodied organs containing a limited variety of housing types that was self-contained in terms of commerce, education and leisure services. The town is a cluster of neighboring units assembled around a civic center with municipal institutions. The developing town aggregates modular units, thus preserving its neighborly character. The size of each unit was determined in relation to the estimated capacity of schools and kindergartens, the optimal dimensions of the commercial center, and the desirable length of paths in the neighborhood. The units were planned in a way that would separate motor traffic from pathways within the neighborhood, enabling pedestrian access to all daily services at a distance of up to 250 meters without having to cross the street.

The smooth, plexing lines of the units, the abundance of open space within and between them, the placement of education and recreation facilities at the heart of the units amidst lawns or woods, the distancing of industrial areas from living quarters and their separation by green belts, the design of repetitive social housing on undivided land, rather than normative parceling and speculative construction—all these forge the most deceptive illusion of all: the new Israeli town was meant to be a blown-up kibbutz based on a homogeneous community, collective and egalitarian, without private capital or unanticipated market forces. However, unlike the kibbutz, or even the pre-State Workers' Housing Co-operative in the well-established towns, which were created as exclusive and hegemonic structures by and for the members of a social avant-garde movement, the New Town came into being superficially and coercively—a professional and bureaucratic doctrine forced upon a population of unsuspecting newcomers used as passive subjects in a national experiment.

With the foundation of the first New Towns, it became apparent that the progressive zoning principles and the generous 'ecological' aptitude simply did not work. The detached, sparsely populated, ready-made towns weighed disproportionately on the national budget due to the huge amounts of infrastructure they demanded. The supply of capital and entrepreneurship (both from public and private sources) required the creation of jobs in those out-of-the-way locations and lagged behind the pace at which the immigrants were sent to the New Towns (in Kiryat Shmona, for instance, the first factory was built a full decade after the town was created). The veteran urban population remained in the cities and ignored the national challenge. The veteran agrarian population of the kibbutzim already had a well-organized marketing network of its own (including such monopolistic co-operatives as Tnuva and Hamashbir) and had no use for the services provided by New Towns, and completely discounted the planners' regionalist vision. The vast expanses that had been water-colored green on paper were totally incongruent with the climate, the water resources and the maintenance facilities in the country, and in reality became dead zones, severing the urban fabric. The autonomous, inward-looking units and the separation of motorways and pedestrian paths obstructed the development of street-life. The 'alienation, degeneration and low quality of life' in the big city, so consistently denounced by official state propaganda, were replaced in no time with homogeneity, remoteness, and deprivation. Criticism soon took over the prophetic positivism of the professionals. During a retrospective discussion on the planning of the New Towns that took place in 1964, architect Yitzhak Yashar concluded: 'There was an industrial world, there were enormous cities, but they sought dispersal there. It was in the center of London—where you cannot go in and you cannot go out, where traffic and noise are tremendous, where there is neither sunlight nor greenery—that the concept was born. The very same idea—not only in its qualitative but also in the quantitative sense, in its formal sense—was shifted to Beersheba. And in Beersheba, where one searches longingly for traffic and commotion, for a bit of social gathering—there, in the middle of the desert, we solved the problems of London [...] but obviously, what is good for five or eight or ten million people is catastrophic when you have a mere ten thousand in the desert.'[10]

Fifty years after its official publication, the Sharon Plan remains valid. The vision of colonization and modernization laid out by the Plan has, for the most part, been implemented. The country has developed at an unprecedented rate of growth. The New Towns —a well-intentioned hybrid of imported urban theories and physiocratic local ideology—still exist more or less as they had originated: barren garden cities, lethargic work towns, bypassed regional centers, homogeneous melting pots, underdeveloped urban odds and ends still struggling to preserve their special Class A tax-reduction status, granted by the various governments to 'areas of national preference.' Just as the citizens of these New Towns played a historic role in realizing the logistic reversal of the 1950s, they have fueled the so-called political turnabout of the 1970s (when the Labor Party lost its hegemony for the first time) and the cultural revolution of the 1990s. With each metamorphosis, their distance from the heart of the country only increased. However, the Israeli cultural and territorial vortex is still sweltering. Once the big sell-out and redevelopment of state-owned agricultural lands is over, and once the political settlements beyond the Green Line are forced to return to the legal boundaries of the state, the peripheral garden cities of yesterday will undoubtedly become the most desirable land reserves: the last option for suburban 'quality of life' so revered by a society that never really coped with its own socialist-agrarian rhetoric and never really sublimated the values of liberal urban life.

notes:

1. Theodor Herzl, *The Jewish State*, translated by Harry
   Zohn, New York: Herzl Press, 1970. Online version:
   http://www.wzo.org.il/en/resources/view.asp?id=287.
2. David Ben-Gurion, *The War Diary: The War of
   Independence*, 1948–1949, edited by Gershon Rivlin
   and Dr. Elhanan Oren, Tel Aviv: Ministry of Defense
   Publishing, 1982, vol. 3, p. 937 (Hebrew).
3. The Planning Division first operated as part of the
   Ministry of Labor and Construction, until Ben-Gurion
   transferred it to the Prime Minister's Office so that he
   would be able to work with the planners directly.
   Subsequently, the Division moved to the Ministry of
   the Interior, and later formed the foundation for the
   establishment of the Ministry of Housing, even though
   its authorities were divided among the various
   ministries. At the time of writing, there is once again
   talk of establishing a Planning Division in the Prime
   Minister's Office, based on the original Ben-Gurion-
   esque model. One can gauge the importance ascribed
   by Ben-Gurion to national planning given the twelve
   hours weekly he dedicated to it, as opposed to the
   eleven hours weekly dedicated to matters of national
   security.
4. The Planning and Building Law was only enforced in 1965.
5. A fascinating illustration of second thoughts among the
   architects associated with the establishment can be found
   in the words of A. Newman of the Planning Division:
   'Obviously we have long lost the naive belief in the
   automatic regulation of the economic and social
   process. We seem to think that the belief in a single
   planning doctrine, that can grant happiness to everyone,
   is likewise naive. [...] We know that planning has a
   component that stifles life, since a heavy planning
   mechanism tends to suppress the individual.' From
   *Journal of the Association of Architects and Engineers in
   Israel*, January 1953 (Hebrew).
6. Eliezer Brutzkus, 'Transformations in the Network of
   Urban Centers in Israel', *Engineering and Architecture*,
   3, 1964, p. 43 (Hebrew).
7. Arieh Sharon himself, after completing his studies in the
   Bauhaus in 1929 and working in Berlin for two years,
   was invited to the Soviet Union by his former teachers
   Hannes Meyer and Mart Stam to participate in the
   planning of the industrial city of Magnitogorsk.
   Sharon chose to return to Palestine and started his

glorious career here by winning the competitions for planning the Workers' Housing Cooperatives (Me'onot Ovdim) in Tel Aviv.

8. Christaller proposed a mathematical model explaining the deployment of the European population, which analyzed the distances between population centers. According to his theory, while the Great Depression that hit Europe and the United States during the years 1929–1933 caused economic devastation and unemployment in large cities and exclusively agricultural areas, the medium-sized and small towns located in provincial areas and sustaining a mixed economy of agriculture, industry and trade were relatively economically and socially stable.

9. Ibid.

10. Yitzhak Yashar, 'A Discussion of New Towns', *Engineering and Architecture*, 3, 1964, p. 15 (Hebrew).

Moshav Olim Eshta'ol
Jerusalem Corridor, JNF Archive
photographer: A. Milewsky, 1953

5.

Rafi Segal, Eyal Weizman

THE MOUNTAIN
PRINCIPLES OF BUILDING IN HEIGHTS

The West Bank settlement project can be seen as the culmination of Zionism's journey from the plains to the hills. It is a journey that attempted to resolve the paradox embedded in early twentieth-century Zionist spatiality; one that, while seeking the return to the 'promised land', mainly inhabited the plains instead of the historical Judean hills, thus reversing the settlement geography of Biblical times. Braudel's observation that the 'mountains are as a rule a world apart from civilizations, which are urban and lowland achievements'[1] is well suited to the ancient geography of Israel. The mountains of Judea became the breeding ground for an isolated form of monotheism, while the plains, inhabited by the 'invaders from the seas', close to the international road system and the seaports, gave birth to an integrative culture set apart from the isolation of the mountains. The Zionist movement, now itself an 'invader from the seas', modern, socialist and pragmatic, settled mainly along the coastal plains and fertile northern valleys, a settlement distribution which suited its ideology of agricultural cultivation. This spatial pattern dominated the Israeli landscape until the political turnabout of 1977 in which the hawkish Likud party replaced Labor in government for the first time.

The topography of the West Bank is easily identified as three long strips of land running from north to south. The most eastern, and topographically the lowest, is the sparsely populated Jordan Valley; west of it rise the high and steep mountains of Judea and Samaria along whose main ridge most large Palestinian cities are located. Further west are the green and fertile slopes of Judea and Samaria. With their moderate topography, agricultural soil, plentiful water and a position overlooking the coastal plain, they form the West Bank's 'area of high demand'.[2] It is in this strip that most Palestinian villages and Jewish settlements are located.

In a strange and almost perfect correlation between latitude, political ideology and urban form, each topographical strip became an arena for another phase of the settlement project, promoted by politicians with different agendas to appeal to settlers of different ideologies in different settlement typologies. The 'civilian occupation' of the West Bank was a process that began in the deep and arid Jordan Valley during the first years of Israeli rule under Labor governments (1967–1977). During that period fifteen agricultural villages were built in an attempt to bring the kibbutz and moshav[3] movements back to the forefront of

Zionism. They were constructed according to the Allon Plan[4] that sought to establish a security border with Jordan while relying on the principle of 'maximum security and maximum territory for Israel, with a minimum number of Arabs'. As the political climate in Israel changed, the topographical migration—a vertical movement from the lowlands to the mountains—coincided with the development of transcendental sentiments and a feeling of acting in accordance with a divine plan. Settlements began a long and steady climb to the mountains, where they were scattered as isolated dormitory communities on barren hilltops, and without the agricultural hinterlands they cultivated nothing but 'holiness'.

The second strip, that of the mountain ridge, began to be settled en masse mainly after the political turnabout of 1977. It was primarily Gush Emunim,[5] a national-religious organization that fused 'Biblical' messianism and a belief in the 'Land of Israel' with political thinking, that allowed for no territorial concessions. Thereafter the Gush pushed the various governments to establish even more new settlements in the mountain region, in and around the Palestinian cities. The settlements of the mountain strip shifted the stimulus of expansion from agricultural pioneering to mysticism and transcendentalism. Beyond the security aspect of these settlements, the climb from the plains to the hills was argued with the rhetoric of the 'regeneration of the soul', as acts of 'personal and national renewal', imbued with the mystic quality of the heights. With respect to the mountains, and in opposition to any dismantling of settlements, Effi Eitam, a retired general and currently the Minister for Infrastructure and head of the National Religious Party, recently announced that 'Whoever proposes that we return to the lowlands, to our lowest levels, to the sands, to the secular, and that it is the very sacred summits that we are to leave in foreign hands, is proposing something senseless.'[6]

The third strip is the one closest to Israel's pre-1967 border. It consists mainly of settlers seeking a better quality of life. The settlements there are in effect garden suburbs that belong to the greater metropolitan areas of Tel Aviv, and consist mainly of private developments. Unlike the ideological settlements that inhabited the mountain ridge of the West Bank, it was the rhetoric of 'living standards', 'quality of life', 'fresh air' and 'open view' that facilitated, mainly in the 1980s, the dissemination of these suburban settlements. For the price of a small apartment in Tel

Aviv, settlers could purchase their own red-roofed house and benefit from massive government subsidies.[7]

The Vertical Perspective

Shortly after the end of the 1967 war, when a new and previously unimagined extent of territory lay in the hands of the Israeli army, a special double-lens aerial camera[8] capable of registering stereoscopic images was acquired, and a series of photographic sorties was launched. The stereoscopic camera is designed to capture two simultaneous images at a slight angle from each other. When viewed through a special optical instrument, the shades of gray on the two flat images are transformed by the gaze of the intelligence analyst into a three-dimensional illusion of depth, reproducing a tabletop model of the pilot's vertical perspective.[9] Knowledge of the West Bank was primarily gathered from the air in this way.[10] Photometrical land surveying from aerial photography, reproduced at variable scales and with breathtaking clarity, replaced the conventional land-surveyed maps as the most rapid and practical way of representing the territory.

This mapping was the end result of an intensive process of photography, analysis and classification, one in which the terrain was charted and mathematicized, topographical lines drafted, slope gradients calculated, built areas and land use marked. The process was so complete and rapid that at the time the West Bank must have been one of the most intensively observed and photographed terrains in the world. The massive project was undertaken not as an objective study but as an act of establishing national ownership that anticipated a spatial reality yet to come.

The mountain peaks of the West Bank easily lent themselves to state seizure. In the absence of an ordered land registry during the period of Jordanian rule, uncultivated land could be declared by Israel as 'state land'.[11] Since Palestinian cultivated lands are found mainly on the slopes and in the valleys, where the agriculturally suitable alluvial soils erode down from the limestone slopes of the West Bank peaks, the barren hilltops, clearly visible on the aerial photographs, could be seized by the state. The result, in sum, left about 40 per cent of the West Bank, composed of a patchwork quilt of isolated plots and discontinuous islands around peaks, in Israeli hands.[12]

The West Bank was thus divided across its vertical axis. In almost every area the hilltops were annexed to Israel de facto, while the valleys between them were left under Palestinian ownership. As intelligence analysts gave way to cartographers and planners, the stereoscopic images became the primary tool with which topographical lines were drawn on maps and, on occasion, even provided the slate for the design work itself.

The process of settlement construction starts with planning on top of an orthogonal-photographic map (ortho-photo)[13] or a topographical map at a scale of 1:1250. Since the construction of the mountain settlements necessitated building in areas with steep slopes and special morphological formations, the terrain was divided into separate topographical conditions and to each was allocated a distinct settlement typology.[14] In the formal processes which base mountain settlements on topographical conditions, the laws of erosion were absorbed into the practice of urban design. The form laid out by nature in the specific summit morphology became the blueprint of development.

The mountain settlement is typified by a principle of concentric organization in which the topographical contours of the map are retraced as lines of infrastructure. The roads are laid out in rings around the summit with the water, sewage, electricity and telephone lines buried under them. The division of lots is equal and repetitive, providing small private red-roofed houses positioned along the roads, against the backdrop of the landscape. The public functions are generally located within the inner most ring, on the highest ground. The 'ideal' arrangement for a small settlement is a circle. However, in reality the geometry of the plan is distorted by the insistent demands of a highly irregular topography, as well as by the extent and form of available state land. Rather than exhibits of ordered forms, settlements are usually manifestations of anti-forms, the end results of tactical, land-use and topographical constraints. Socially, the 'community settlement', a new settlement typology introduced in the early 1980s for the West Bank, is in effect an exclusive members' club with a long admission process and a monitoring mechanism that regulates everything from religious observance through ideological rigor. Furthermore, they function as dormitory suburbs for small communities which travel to work in the large Israeli cities. The hilltop environment, isolated, overseeing and hard to reach, lent itself to the development of this newly conceived form of 'utopia.' The community settlements create cul-de-sac envelopes, closed off from their surroundings, utopian in their concentric organization, promoting a mythic communal coherence in a shared formal identity. It is the externally enclosed and internally oriented layout of homes which promotes the inner social vision and facilitates the close managing of daily life.

Shortly after Matityahu Drobles was appointed the head of the Jewish Agency's Land Settlement Division in 1978, he issued *The Master Plan for the Development of Settlements in Judea and Samaria*,[15] in which he declared that 'Settlement throughout the whole Land of Israel is for security and by right. A belt of settlements in strategic locations increases both internal and external security [...] therefore, the proposed settlement blocs are spread out as a belt surrounding the mountains, starting along the western slopes [of the Samaria Mountains] from north to south, and along the eastern slopes from south to north, within the minority population as well as surrounding it ...'. 'Being bisected by Jewish settlements,' Drobles explains on another occasion, 'the minority population will find it hard to create unification and territorial contiguity.' Drobles's master plan, outlining possible locations for scores of new settlements, aimed to achieve its political goals by way of a reorganization of space. Relying heavily on the topographical nature of the West Bank, he proposed that new high-volume traffic arteries, connecting Israel to the West Bank and beyond, should be stretched along the large west-draining valleys and that, for their security, new settlement blocs should be placed on the hilltops along their route. Furthermore, he proposed to locate settlements on the summits surrounding the large Palestinian cities and alongside the roads connecting them.

Optical Planning

High ground offers three strategic assets: greater tactical strength, self-protection and a wider view, which are principles as old as military history itself. Like the Crusaders' fortresses, some incidentally built on the West Bank summits, settlements operate through 'the reinforcement of strength already provided by nature'.[16] The settlements are not only places of residence, but create a large-scale network of 'civilian fortifications', generating tactical territorial surveillance in the state's regional strategic defense plan. But unlike in the fortresses and military camps of previous periods, the actual fortification work is absent in the settlements. Up until recent times, only a few mountain settlements were surrounded by walls or fences, as settlers argued that their homes must form a continuity with 'their' landscapes, that they were not foreign invaders in need of protection, but rather that the Palestinians were those who needed to be fenced in. The fact that during the time of the current Palestinian uprising many settlements have been attacked generated debates concerning the use, effect and moral significance of walls and fences. Extremist settlers claimed that, besides the aspect of the 'open panorama', defense could be implemented through the power of vision,[17] rendering the material protection of a fortified wall redundant and, in cases of a solid wall, even obstructive.[18]

In 1984 the Ministry of Construction and Housing published a guideline for new construction in the mountain regions. It was in effect a building manual for the construction of settlements in the West Bank. One of the main concerns of this manual is the view. One typical phrase advises architects that, 'turning openings in the direction of the view is usually identical with turning them in the direction of the slope. [The optimal view depends on] the positioning of the buildings and on the distances between them, on the density, the gradient of the slope and the vegetation.'[19] Urban layout that follows topographical lines around the mountain summit is contingent with the principle of maximizing the view. A clear view of the surrounding landscape is easily achieved for homes inhabiting the outermost ring. The homes in the inner rings are positioned accordingly in line with the gaps left between the homes in the outer one. This outward-looking arrangement of homes around summits imposes on the dwellers axial visibility (and lateral invisibility) oriented in two directions: inward and outward. The inward oriented gaze protects the soft cores of the settlements, and the outward oriented one surveys the landscape around it.

With respect to the interior of each building, the guideline recommends the orientation of the bedrooms towards the inner public spaces, and that of the living rooms towards the distant view. Vision dictated the discipline of design and its methodologies on all scales. Regionally, a strategic function was integrated into the distribution of settlements across the entire territory, creating a 'network of observation' that overlooks the main traffic arteries of the West Bank; topographically, it was integrated into the siting of the settlements on summits; urbanistically it was integrated into their very layout, as rings around the summit, and in the positioning of homes perpendicular to the slope; architecturally, it was integrated into the arrangements and orientation of rooms, and finally into the precise positioning of windows. As if, following Paul Virilio, 'the function of arms and the function of the eye were indefinitely identified as one and the same'.[20]

Indeed, the form of the mountain settlements is constructed according to the laws of a geometric system that unites the effectiveness of sight with that of spatial order, thereby producing sight-lines that function to achieve different forms of power: strategic in its overlooking of main traffic arteries, controlling in its overlooking of Palestinian towns and villages, and self-defensive in its overlooking its immediate surroundings and approach roads. Settlements become, in effect, optical devices, designed to exercise control through supervision and surveillance.

Responding to mathematical layouts and maximizing visibility across the landscape means that power, just as in Michel Foucault's description of Jeremy Bentham's Panopticon,[21] could be exercised through observation. In his verdict supporting the 'legality' of settlements, Israeli High Court Justice Alfred Vitkon, while arguing for the strategic importance of a settlement, declared: 'With respect to pure military considerations, there is no doubt that the presence of settlements, even if "civilian", of the occupying power in the occupied territory, substantially contributes to the security in that area and facilitates the execution of the duties of the military. One does not have to be an expert in military and security affairs to understand that terrorist elements operate more easily in an area populated only by an indifferent population or one that supports the enemy, as opposed to an area in which there are persons who are likely to observe them and inform the authorities about any suspicious movement. Among them no refuge, assistance, or equipment will be provided to terrorists. The matter is simple, and details are unnecessary.'[22]

What becomes evident is that by placing settlers across the landscape, the Israeli government is not merely utilizing the agencies of state power and control, namely the police and army, for the administration of power, but that it 'drafts' the civilian population to inspect, control and subdue the Palestinian population. An inconsistency develops between what the settlers want to see, the way they describe and understand the panorama, and the way that their eyes are 'hijacked' for the strategic and geopolitical aims of the state. The desire for a single family home is being mobilized to serve the quest for military domination, while an act of domesticity, shrouded in the cosmetic facade of red tiles and green lawns, provides visual territorial control.

The Horizontal Panorama

The journey to the mountain tops sought to re-establish the tie between terrain and sacred text by tracing the location of 'Biblical' sites and constructing settlements adjacent to them. Settlers turned topography into sceneography, forming an exegetical landscape with a mesh of scriptural signification that must be extracted from the panorama and 'read' rather than merely be 'seen'. A settlement located near the Palestinian city of Nablus advertises itself thus: 'Shilo spreads up the hills overlooking Tel Shilo [Shilo Mound], where over 3,000 years ago the Children of Israel gathered to erect the Tabernacle and to divide by lot the Land of Israel into tribal portions [...] This ancient spiritual center has retained its power as the focus of modern day Shilo.'[23] No longer seen as a resource to be agriculturally or industrially cultivated, the landscape, imbued with imaginary religious signifiers, established the link that helped re-create and re-enact religious-national myths that displace (on the very same land) ancient with modern time. This romantic 'Biblical' panorama does not evoke solemn contemplation, but produces an active staring, a part of a religious ritual that causes a sensation of sheer ecstasy. 'It causes me excitement that I cannot even talk about in modesty,'[24] said Menora Katzover, the daughter of a prominent settlers' leader, about the view of the Samaria Mountains. Another sales brochure, for the ultra-Orthodox settlement of Emanuel, published in Brooklyn for member recruitment,[25] evokes the picturesque: 'The city of Emanuel, situated 440 meters above sea level, has a magnificent view of the coastal plain and the Judean Mountains. The hilly landscape is dotted by green olive orchards and enjoys a pastoral calm.'

In the ideal image of the pastoral landscape, integral to the perspective of colonial traditions, the admiration of the rustic panorama is always viewed through the window frames of modernity. The impulse to retreat from the city to the country reasserts the virtues of a simpler life close to nature. It draws on the opposition between luxury and simplicity, the spontaneous and the planned, nativity and foreignness, which are nothing but the opposite poles of the axis of vision that stretches between the settlements and their surrounding landscape. Furthermore, the re-creation of the picturesque scenes of a Biblical landscape becomes a testimony to an ancient claim on the land. The admiration of the landscape thus functions as a cultural practice, by which social and subjective identities are formed.

Within this panorama, however, lies a cruel paradox: the very thing that renders the landscape 'Biblical' or 'pastoral', its traditional inhabitation and cultivation in terraces, olive orchards, stone buildings and the presence of livestock, is produced by the Palestinians, whom the Jewish settlers came to replace. And yet, the very people who cultivate the 'green olive orchards' and render the landscape Biblical are themselves excluded from the panorama. The Palestinians are there to produce the scenery and then disappear. It is only when talking about the roads that the Palestinians are mentioned in the brochure, and then only by way of exclusion: 'A motored system is being developed that will make it possible to travel quickly and safely to the Tel Aviv area and to Jerusalem on modern throughways, by-passing Arab towns.'[26] The gaze that sees a 'pastoral, Biblical landscape' does not register what it does not want to see, it is a visual exclusion that seeks a physical exclusion. Like a theatrical set, the panorama can be seen as an edited landscape put together by invisible stage hands that must step off the set as the lights come on. The panoptic arrangement of sight-lines therefore serves two contradictory agendas: supervision and a self-imposed scotoma. What for the state is a supervision mechanism that seeks to observe the Palestinians is for the settlers a window on to a pastoral landscape that seeks to erase them. The Jewish settlements superimpose another datum of latitudinal geography upon an existing landscape. Settlers can thus see only other settlements, avoid those of the Palestinian towns and villages, and feel that they have truly arrived 'as the people without land to the land without people'.[27]

Latitude has become more than the mere relative position on the folded surface of the terrain. It literally functions to establish parallel geographies of 'First' and 'Third' Worlds that inhabit two distinct planar strata in the startling and unprecedented proximity that only the vertical dimension of the mountains could provide. The landscape does not simply signify power relations, but functions as an instrument of domination and control. The extreme relationship that developed between politics, strategy and building practices within the topography of the West Bank exposes the terrifying role of the most ubiquitous of architectural typologies. Rather than the conclusive, binary division between two nations across a boundary line, the organization of the West Bank has created multiple separations and provisional boundaries that relate to one another through surveillance and control, an intensification and ramification of power that could be achieved in this form only because of the particularity of the terrain. By strategically overlooking the valleys where most Palestinian villages are located, the settlements precipitated the creation of two parallel and self-referential ethno-national geographies that manifest themselves along the vertical axis in the physical 'above' and 'below'.

In memory of Paul Hirst

notes:

1. Fernand Braudel, *The Mediterranean and the Mediterranean World in the Age of Philip II*, Berkeley and Los Angeles: University of California Press, 1995, p. 34.
2. The main characteristic of the Western Hills is their proximity to the main urban centers on Israel's coastal plain. In the development plan for 1983–1986, this strip was defined as the 'area of high demand' because of the short travel times (twenty to thirty minutes) from there to the employment centers inside Israel. See Yehezkel Lein & Eyal Weizman, *Land Grab: Israel's Settlement Policy in the West Bank*, Jerusalem: B'Tselem, May 2002, especially pp. 90–93 (draft published online at www.btselem.org).
3. Kibbutz and moshav are co-operative agricultural settlement typologies that were promoted by Socialist Zionism even prior to the establishment of the State of Israel.

4. As early as the end of 1967, Yigal Allon, who served at the
   time as the head of the Ministerial Committee on
   Settlements, began to prepare a strategic plan for the
   establishment of settlements in the West Bank. Although
   never formally approved by the Israeli government, the
   plan provided the basis for the location of the
   settlements up until 1977, and as the foundation for the
   'territorial compromise' advocated by the Labor Party.
   The initial objective of the Allon Plan was to redraw the
   borders of the State of Israel to include the Jordan
   Valley and the Judean Desert in order to facilitate the
   military defense of Israel. Within these areas, the plan
   advocated the establishment of a string of Israeli
   settlements ensuring a 'Jewish presence' and constituting
   a preliminary step leading to formal annexation. The
   Allon Plan also recommended that, as far as possible, the
   settlement and the annexation of areas densely populated
   by Palestinians should be avoided.
5. Gush Emunim ('The Bloc of Faith') was established in
   1974 following the Yom Kippur War under the spiritual
   leadership of Rabbi Zvi Yehuda Kook.
6. Ari Shavit, *A Leader Awaits a Signal*, *Haaretz*, Friday
   Supplement, 22 March 2002, p. 20 (Hebrew).
7. All Israeli governments have implemented a vigorous and
   systematic policy to encourage Israeli citizens to move
   from Israel to the West Bank. One of the main tools used
   to realize this policy is the provision of significant
   financial benefits and incentives. See Lein & Weizman,
   Land Grab, pp. 60–72.
8. The double-lens aerial camera was an RC-8 with a format
   of 24 cms^2.
9. Stereoscopic image-making has its roots in seventeenth-
   century Italy with the binocular drawings of Giovanni
   Battista della Porta. As a photographic technique it was
   developed in 1838 by Sir Charles Wheatstone in England
   and was quickly popularized across Europe as a kind of
   salon-tourism. It was first used as a reconnaissance
   technique by the Royal Air Force in World War II.
10. On the process of aerial mapping of the West Bank and
    Israel, see also Moshe Saban, 'Aerial Photography and
    Photometrics,' in Amiram Harlap Architect, ed., *Israel
    Builds*, Jerusalem: Ministry of Construction and
    Housing, 1988, p. 53.
11. This is based on a manipulative use of the Ottoman Land
    Law of 1858, according to which a person may secure
    ownership of land by holding and working it for
    ten consecutive years. If the land was not farmed for
    three consecutive years the state could take possession of

it. By this method, approximately 40 per cent of the area of the West Bank was declared state land. Approximately 90 per cent of the settlements were established on state lands, and the remaining lands were seized by other means. See Lein & Weizman, *Land Grab*, pp. 37–40.

12. See the Regional Council Jurisdictional Areas on the 'Israeli Settlements in the West Bank' map pp. 112–119.

13. The Orthogonal Photographic Map is an aerial photograph where lens distortions are accounted and compensated for. Further information may then be overlaid, most commonly in the form of topographical lines and roads.

14. The steeper the land, the further away from agriculture the settlement. Small agricultural settlements were recommended for gradient of 15–25 per cent, suburban settlements for 25–50 per cent, while towns were recommended for gradient of 50 per cent and over.

15. Matityahu Drobles, *Masterplan for the Development of Settlement in Judea and Samaria for the Years 1979–1983,* Jerusalem: The Jewish Agency-Settlement Division, 1979 (Hebrew).

16. R. C. Smail, *Crusading Warfare*, 1097–1193, Cambridge: Cambridge University Press, 1995, p. 217.

17. Qedumim is one of the settlements that has no fence for ideological reasons. 'Fences project a sense of fear to the Arabs, it stops the settlement from widening and it's definitely not working as a security measure,' said its security officer. Instead, additional surveillance stations and cameras were placed for this aim: 'The layout of the settlement and the design of its houses are a part of a security system, to this we add the electronic eyes— state of the art surveillance equipment, equipped with night-vision capability that homes in on movement.' Both quotes are from Shlomi Hazoni, the security officer of Qedumim, in an interview with Mira Asseo, November 2002. Mira Asseo is a researcher for Eyal Weizman and Nadav Harel's documentary, *The Politics of Verticality.*

18. See the article by Sharon Rotbard, *Homa Umigdal*, in this book, pp. 39–56. Whereas the historical precedent for fortified Zionist settlements could be found with the Wall and Tower settlements of *Homa Umigdal* that relies on the physical fortification of a wall, these were mainly designed for a flat landscape in the northern plains of Israel. To enable distant views, a tower was required. In the Jewish settlements of the mountainous West Bank, home windows have a compounded double function that includes a ramification of both the function of the tower as well as that of the wall. This is made

possible, of course, because settlements were built on
the hilltops.

19. M. Boneh, *Building and Development in the Mountain
Regions*, Government of Israel, Jerusalem: Ministry of
Construction and Housing, May 1984, p. 14 (Hebrew).

20. Paul Virilio, *Bunker Archeologie*, Paris: Les Éditions
du Demi-Circle, 1994, p. 17.

21. See Michel Foucault, *Discipline and Punish: The Birth of
the Prison*, London: Penguin Books, 1991, pp. 179–207.

22. HCJ 834/78, *Salameh et al v. Minister of Defense et al*,
Piskei Din 33(1) 971;Beth El; p. 119.

23. www.shilo.co.il as of 4 April 2002.

24. Daniel Ben Simon, *It is Strange to Die after the Second
Meeting*, *Haaretz*, Friday Supplement, 29 March 2002,
p. 5 (Hebrew).

25. The brochure is titled 'Emanuel, A Faithful City in
Israel', The Emanuel Office, Brooklyn, NYC.

26. It is worth nothing that the use of the term 'Arabs'
for the Palestinian Arabs is not politically innocent.
The settlers do not recognize the Palestinians as
belonging to a separate Arab nation.

27. This famous slogan is attributed to Israel Zangwill,
who arrived in Palestine before the time of the British
Mandate. The slogan described the land to which
Eastern European Zionism was headed as desolate
and forsaken.

right: Na'hliel, Ramallah region
photograph: Milutin Labudovic for Peace Now, 2002

next page: Na'ale, Gush Modi'im
photograph: Eyal Weizman, 2002

6.

Rafi Segal, Eyal Weizman

THE BATTLE FOR THE HILLTOPS

Beginning at the end of the Rabin government and lasting to the present day, the 'battle for the hilltops' (fought against both Palestinians and Israeli governments) was conducted by settlers in order to capture and settle as many strategic hilltops as possible in the West Bank. Sometimes organized, sometimes acting as individuals, settlers established about 100 'temporary' outposts with a total population of about 1,000, dwelling in mobile homes. They were settled without owning the land, against the law and military orders. The outposts are located on hilltops overlooking the landscapes surrounding the roads leading to the settlements, in close proximity to them. Named by their latitude as marked on topographical maps (e.g. 'Hill 777' or 'Hill 851') they are mere 'facts on the ground' set in the belief that Jewish inhabitation will transform the settlement project from a collection of isolated points in an Arab area to a continuous Jewish territory, demarcating the future border to Israel's advantage.

One of the most influential rabbis of the settlements, Rabbi Yaakov Medan, exclaimed: 'We move forward and beat the enemy with an increased control of the open terrain … the outposts gave us the reason of being and the reason for holding fast to this good and hard mountain … Giving up the outposts is akin to giving up our right to hold the terrain or the line, and to a claim that we hold nothing but points …' (Nekuda 255, September 2002)

Young and extremely ideological and religious settlers responded to the prompt calls of the then opposition leader Ariel Sharon, who encouraged them to 'move, run and grab as many hilltops as you can to enlarge the Jewish settlements because everything we take now will stay ours … everything we don't grab will go to them.' The so-called 'kids of the hills', rarely beyond their teens, rejected the suburban culture of their settlements and replaced it with a strong sense of the wild frontier that seemed at times influenced, in its urban form, or in their own self-image of idealistic and law-breaking heroes on horseback, by Hollywood Westerns. In contrast to the suburban economy of the settlements, the outposts seek Biblical self-sustainability based on shepherding, manual labor and agriculture—either self-cultivated or the harvesting by force of Palestinian crops.

Sometimes, in search of the government's approval, strange techniques are invented. The outpost of Migron was established after settlers asked for a cellular telephone antenna (for better reception) to be placed on a hilltop nearby. The expensive antenna had to be guarded. A guard was brought in, but as he was religious another ten were brought in to allow him to pray according to basic Talmudic law. Today Migron is home to twenty families.

These photographs were taken for the Peace Now (Shalom Achshav) organization as part of a large-scale territorial survey of illegal settlement activity during 1999.

right: Mitzpe Erez, Jordan Valley region

following pages: p.104: Mitzpe Dani, Jordan Valley Region *p.106*: A new outpost by settlement of Itamar, Nablus region
photographs: Daniel Bauer for Peace Now, 1999

7.

B'Tselem and Eyal Weizman

MAP OF ISRAELI SETTLEMENTS IN THE WEST BANK

This map is an up-to-date description of the Israeli settlement project in the West Bank. It marks the location, size and form of Israeli settlements, the scope of their potential expansion, and the total amount of state land at their disposal.

The map is the outcome of a long process of collection, analysis and synthesis of a large number of maps, plans and geographical data. The information was difficult to obtain. It usually demanded travel to individual settlements, sometimes even legal action against refusal to deliver what should in principle be public documents open to public scrutiny and to a due process of planning objections.

The map describes the West Bank as an interwoven patchwork of alienated ethno-national enclaves. It clearly demonstrates how the Israeli settlement project created a new geography in the heart of the Palestinian one.

The precise location markings and formal layout of settlements displayed on the map help in understanding the territorial paradox that asks how, with a built fabric of less than 2 per cent of the total land of the West Bank, settlements have managed to achieve a complete fragmentation and control of the entire territory.

What is charted on the map as an outcome was already clearly drawn as intentions and projections in the plans of the late 1970s and early 1980s. Then, settlement location strategy was directed by the self-proclaimed aim of bisecting and squeezing out Palestinian communities, or else by using Israeli civilians to supervise vital interests as plain-clothed security personnel.

The fact that this map does not mark the settlements as mere points but describes the actual form of their layout, shows that, beyond the mere presence of Israeli settlements on occupied land, it is the way they have been positioned, designed and laid out that directly and negatively affects the lives and livelihood of Palestinians.

However, the geometry, morphology and organization of matter across the terrain are but momentary states in a process of continuous transformation by military incursions and building expansions. Since settlements can still triple their built fabric and population within their established municipal boundaries, this map, besides describing a present set of affairs outlines, in fact, a possible future.

1.

SETTLERS
IN THE WEST BANK

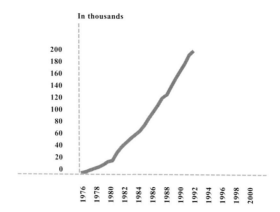

In thousands

2.

CONSTRUCTION
OF HOUSING UNITS
IN THE WEST BANK
AND GAZA STRIP

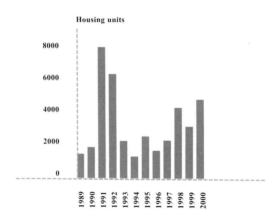

Housing units

3.

NUMBER OF
SETTLEMENTS IN THE
WEST BANK

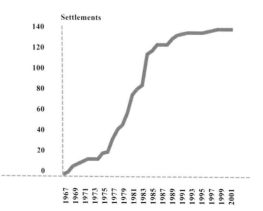

Settlements

Note: Diagrams do not
include East Jerusalem

A.

B.

C.

D.

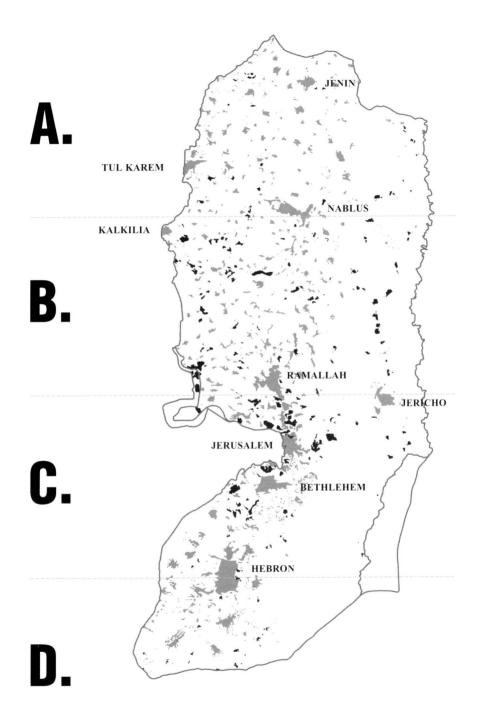

TUL KAREM

KALKILIA

JENIN

NABLUS

RAMALLAH

JERICHO

JERUSALEM

BETHLEHEM

HEBRON

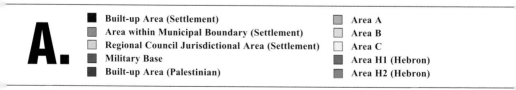

A.

■	Built-up Area (Settlement)	☐ Area A
▨	Area within Municipal Boundary (Settlement)	☐ Area B
☐	Regional Council Jurisdictional Area (Settlement)	☐ Area C
▨	Military Base	■ Area H1 (Hebron)
■	Built-up Area (Palestinian)	▨ Area H2 (Hebron)

112

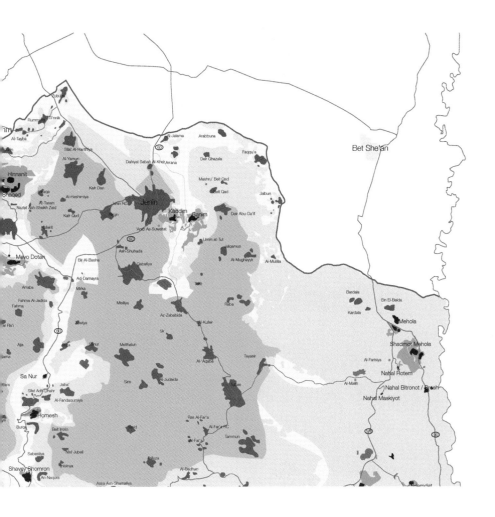

— **Regular Road**   **Abbreviations:**
═ **By-pass Road**   **RC—Refugee Camp**
— **1949 Armistice Line ("Green Line")**   **Kh.—Khirbe—Small Village**
⑥ **Road Number**   **Scale 1:150,000**

```
0  1  2  3  4  5              10 KM
```

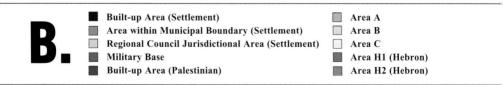

B. ■ Built-up Area (Settlement)
    ■ Area within Municipal Boundary (Settlement)
    □ Regional Council Jurisdictional Area (Settlement)
    ■ Military Base
    ■ Built-up Area (Palestinian)

□ Area A
□ Area B
□ Area C
■ Area H1 (Hebron)
□ Area H2 (Hebron)

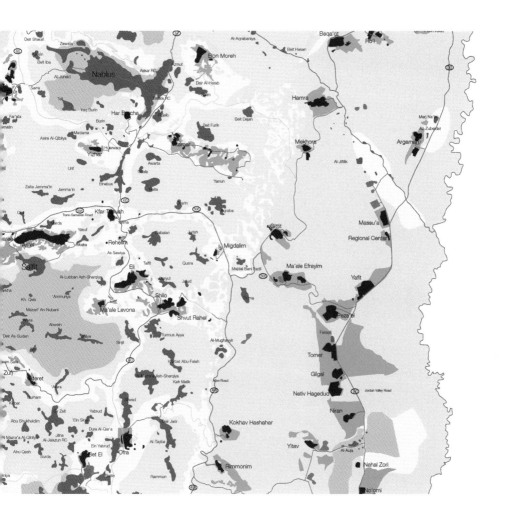

- ━━ **Regular Road**
- ═══ **By-pass Road**
- ━━ **1949 Armistice Line ("Green Line")**
- ⑧⑤ **Road Number**

Abbreviations:
RC—Refugee Camp
Kh.—Khirbe—Small Village
Scale 1:150,000

0 1 2 3 4 5   10 KM

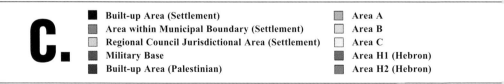

C.

■ Built-up Area (Settlement)	▢ Area A
▨ Area within Municipal Boundary (Settlement)	▢ Area B
▨ Regional Council Jurisdictional Area (Settlement)	▢ Area C
■ Military Base	▨ Area H1 (Hebron)
■ Built-up Area (Palestinian)	▨ Area H2 (Hebron)

116

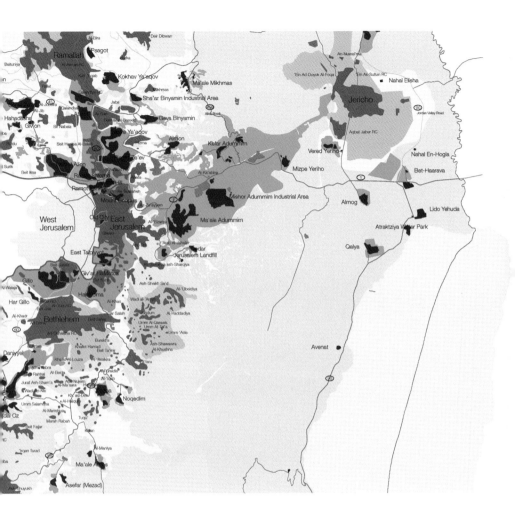

- Regular Road
- By-pass Road
- 1949 Armistice Line ("Green Line")
- ⊚ Road Number

Abbreviations:
RC—Refugee Camp
Kh.—Khirbe—Small Village
Scale 1:150,000

0 1 2 3 4 5   10 KM

117

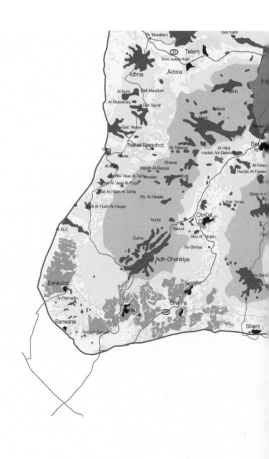

A   B   C   D

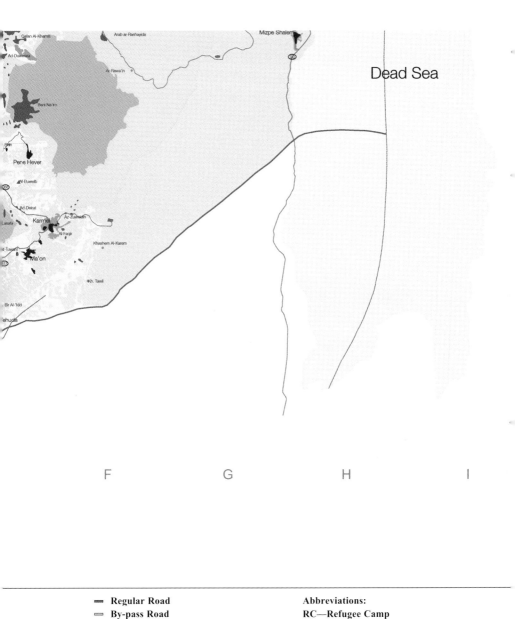

Dead Sea

Qasan Al-Khamis
Arab ar-Rashayida
Mizpe Shalem
Ad-Duwwara
Ar-Rawa'in
Bani Na'im
Brin
Pene Hever
Al-Buwaib
Ad-Deirat
Karmel
Az-Zuweidin
Lasafa
Al-Farjir
At-Tuwana
Khashem Al-Karem
Ma'on
Kh. Tawil
Bir Al-'Idd
Yehuda

F   G   H   I

━ Regular Road
═ By-pass Road
━ 1949 Armistice Line ("Green Line")
⑳ Road Number

Abbreviations:
RC—Refugee Camp
Kh.—Khirbe—Small Village
Scale 1:150,000

0 1 2 3 4 5   10 KM

8.

PLANS OF SETTLEMENTS IN THE WEST BANK

All map locations in this chapter refer to the map
reproduced at pp. 118-19 of this book

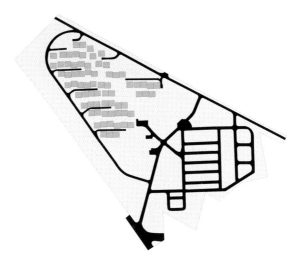

Mehola
Area: Jordan Valley
Population: 300
Established: 1968
Location on map: H3
Latitude: -180
Type: Moshav

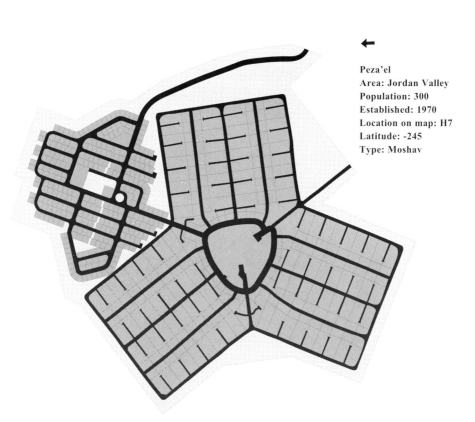

Peza'el
Area: Jordan Valley
Population: 300
Established: 1970
Location on map: H7
Latitude: -245
Type: Moshav

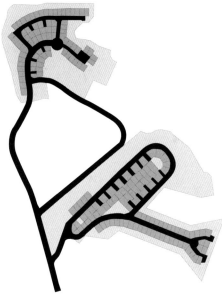

→

Mitzpe Shalem
Area: Dead Sea
Population: 200
Established: 1971
Location on map: H12
Latitude: -320
Type: Kibbutz

←

Hamra
Area: Jordan Valley
Population: 150
Established: 1971
Location on map: H15
Latitude: -55
Type: Moshav

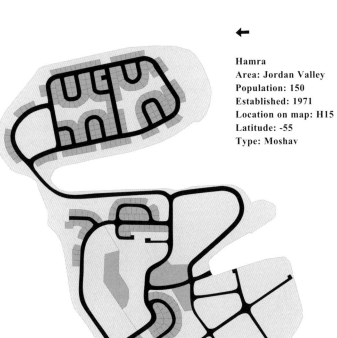

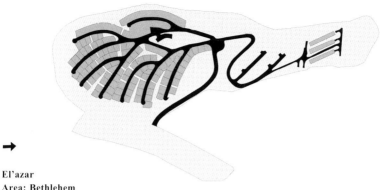

El'azar
Area: Bethlehem
Population: 200
Established: 1975
Location on map: E11
Latitude: 910
Type: Community Settlement
Planner: Settlement Planning Department

Gitit
Area: Jordan valley
Population: 100
Established: 1972
Location on map: G6
Latitude: 305
Type: Moshav

Mechora
Area: Jordan valley
Population: 150
Established: 1973
Location on map: H5
Latitude: 225
Type: Moshav

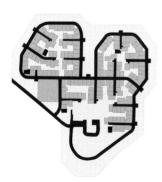

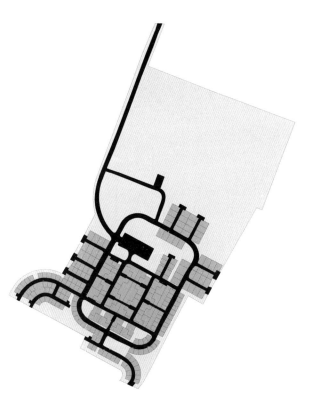

Ro'i
Area: Jordan Valley
Population: 150
Established: 1976
Location on map: H4
Latitude: 30
Type: Moshav

↓

Tomer
Area: Jordan Valley
Population: 300
Established: 1976
Location on map: H7
Latitude: -220
Type: Moshav
Planner: Yiga'al Levy

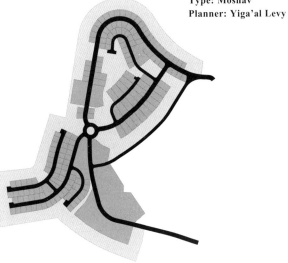

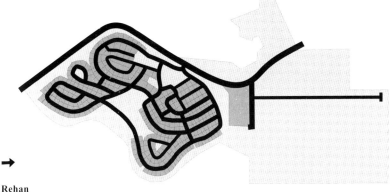

Rehan
Area: Jenin
Population: 120
Established: 1977
Location on map: E2
Latitude: 375
Type: Community Settlement
Planner: A. Inbar, M. Ravid

Beth Horon
Area: Ramallah
Population: 750
Established: 1977
Location on map: E8
Latitude: 620
Type: Community Settlement
Planner: The Settlement
Planning Department

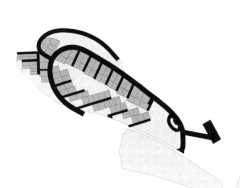

Givon
Area: Ramallah
Population: 1200
Established: 1977
Location on map: E9
Latitude: 755
Type: Community Settlement

↓

Sal'it
Area: Tul Karem
Population: 500
Established: 1977
Location on map: D4
Latitude: 260
Type: Moshav

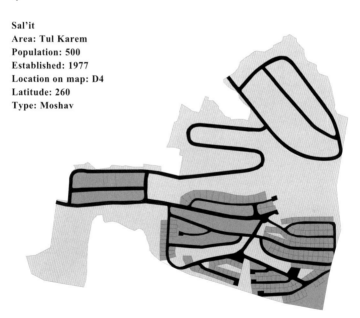

126

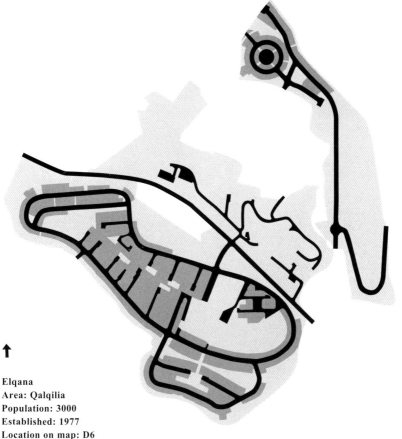

↑

Elqana
Area: Qalqilia
Population: 3000
Established: 1977
Location on map: D6
Latitude: 235
Type: Local council

→

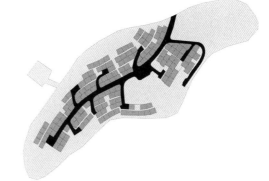

Rimmonim
Area: Jericho
Population: 500
Established: 1977
Location on map: G8
Latitude: 680
Type: Moshav
Planner: The Settlement
Planning Department

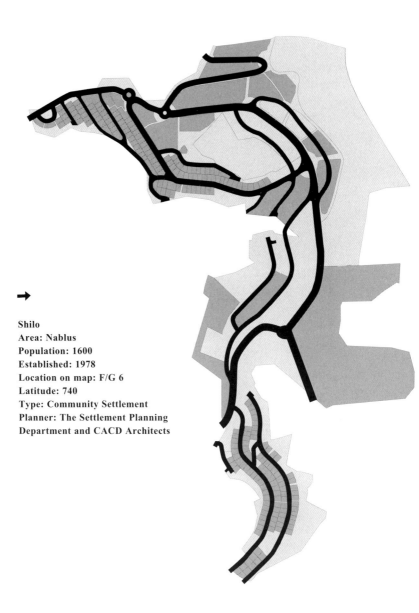

Shilo
Area: Nablus
Population: 1600
Established: 1978
Location on map: F/G 6
Latitude: 740
Type: Community Settlement
Planner: The Settlement Planning
Department and CACD Architects

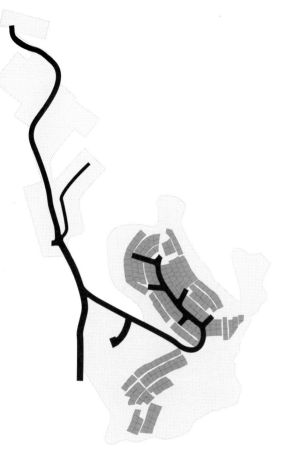

←

Mitzpe Yericho
Area: Jericho
Population: 1200
Established: 1978
Location on map: G9
Latitude: 160
Type: Community Settlement
Planner: The Settlement
Planning Department

➡

Tapuah
Area: Nablus
Population: 350
Established: 1978
Location on map: F6
Latitude: 650
Type: Community Settlement
Planner: M. Ravid

129

→

Elon Moreh
Area: Nablus
Population: 1000
Established: 1979
Location on map: G4
Latitude: 640
Type: Community Settlement
Planner: M. Ravid

↓

Kfar Edummim
Area: Jerusalem
Population: 1700
Established: 1979
Location on map: G9
Latitude: 360
Type: Community Settlement
Planner: Samach-Abramowitz,
Moshe Goldwasser, Gideon Harlap

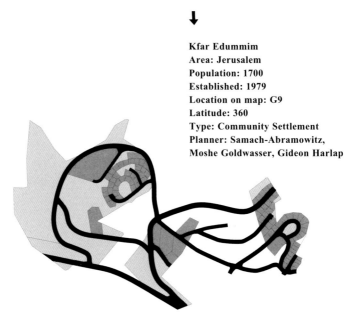

130

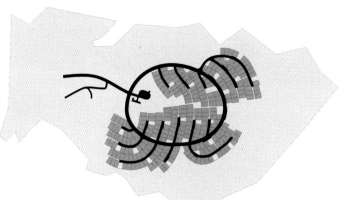

Hinanit
Area: Jenin
Population: 500
Established: 1980
Location on map: E2
Latitude: 385
Type: Community Settlement
Planner: A. Inbar

Nofim
Area: Nablus
Population: 400
Established: 1980
Location on map: E5
Latitude: 380
Type: Community Settlement
Planner: Rachel Walden

Yafit
Area: Jordan Valley
Population:150
Established: 1980
Location on map: H2
Latitude: -245
Type: Moshav

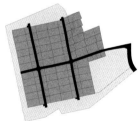

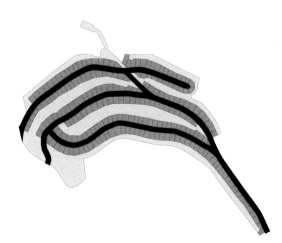

131

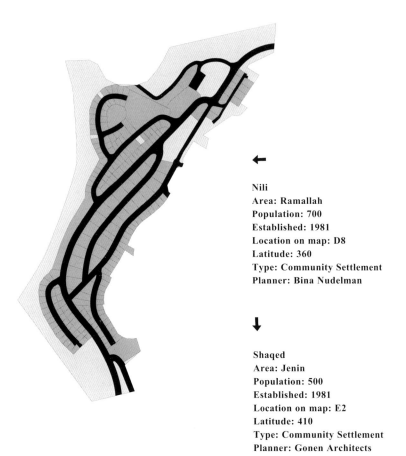

←

Nili
Area: Ramallah
Population: 700
Established: 1981
Location on map: D8
Latitude: 360
Type: Community Settlement
Planner: Bina Nudelman

↓

Shaqed
Area: Jenin
Population: 500
Established: 1981
Location on map: E2
Latitude: 410
Type: Community Settlement
Planner: Gonen Architects

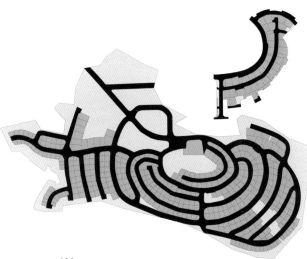

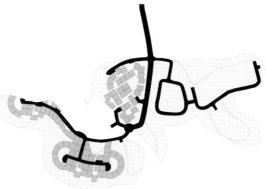

Ma'on
Area: Hebron
Population: 250
Established: 1981
Location on map: E14
Latitude: 770
Type: Community Settlement

Ateret
Area: Ramallah
Population: 300
Established: 1981
Location on map: E7
Latitude: 720
Type: Community Settlement
Planner: S. Melman, A. Kaplan

Hermesh
Area: Jenin
Population: 300
Established: 1982
Location on map: E2
Latitude: 270
Type: Community Settlement
Planner: Shahar Yehoshua

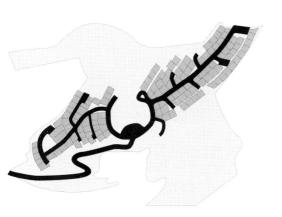

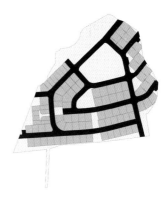

133

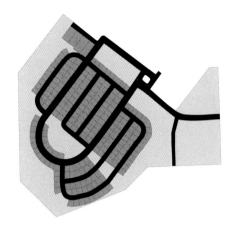

Na'ama
Area: Jordan Valley
Population: 130
Established: 1982
Location on map: H3
Latitude: -200
Type: Moshav

Noqedim
Area: Bethlehem
Population: 600
Established: 1982
Location on map: F11
Latitude: 570
Type: Community Settlement
Planner: The Settlement Division
of the Jewish Agency

134

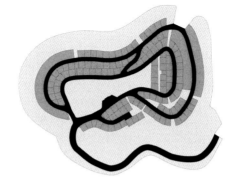

➡

Ma'ale Levona
Area: Nablus
Population: 500
Established: 1982
Location on map: F6
Latitude: 734
Type: Community Settlement
Planner: Rachel Walden

Ganim
Area: Jenin
Population: 100
Established: 1983
Location on map: G2
Latitude: 280
Type: Community Settlement
Planner: M. Ravid, A. Inbar,
Ya'ad Architects

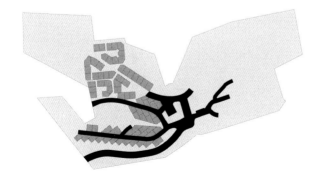

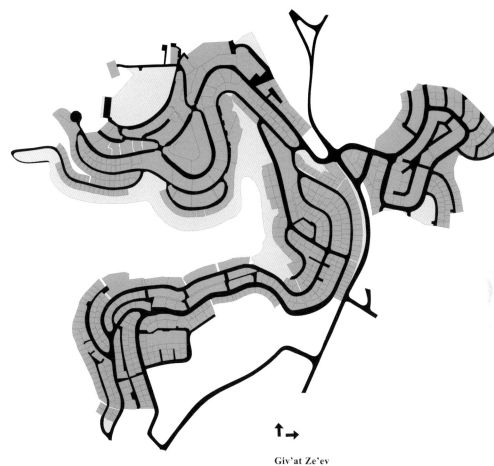

Giv'at Ze'ev
Area: Ramallah
Population: 10,300
Established: 1983
Location on map: E9
Latitude: 760
Type: Local Council
Planner: Nehemya Gorali

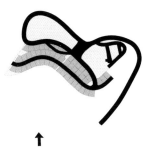

↑

Dolev
Area: Ramallah
Population: 900
Established: 1983
Location on map: E8
Latitude: 600
Type: Community Settlement

↓

Karmei Tzur
Area: Hebron
Population: 500
Established: 1984
Location on map: E11
Latitude: 940
Type: Community Settlement
Planner: The Settlement Division
of the Jewish Agency

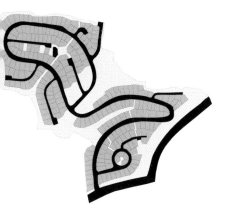

137

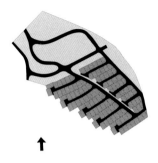

↑

Kohav Yaakov
Area: Ramallah
Population: 2200
Established: 1984
Location on map: F8
Latitude: 765
Type: Community Settlement
Planner: Eyal Itzki

↓

Eli
Area: Nablus
Population: 2500
Established: 1984
Location on map: F6
Latitude: 700
Type: Community Settlement
Planner: The Settlement
Planning Department

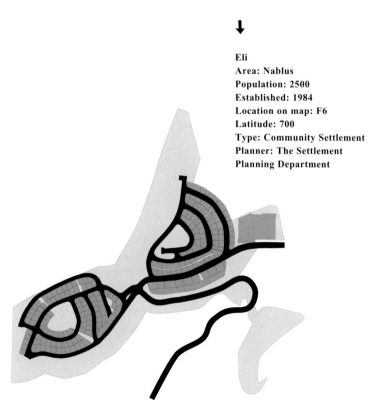

Nahliel
Area: Ramallah
Population: 300
Established: 1984
Location on map: E7
Latitude: 565
Type: Community Settlement

Geva Binyamin
Area: Ramallah
Population: 1000
Established: 1984
Location on map: F9
Latitude: 640
Type: Community Settlement
Planner: The Settlement
Planning Department

↓

Na'ale
Area: Ramallah
Population: 150
Established: 1985
Location on map: D8
Latitude: 430
Type: Community Settlement
Planner: A. Wizenthal

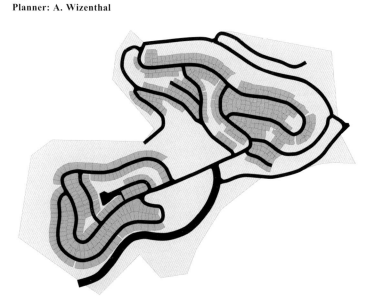

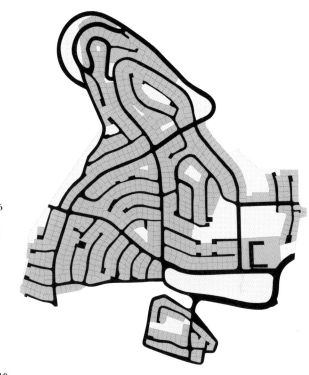

Oranit
Area: Jenin
Population: 5000
Established: 1985
Location on map: D6
Latitude: 140
Type: Local Council

Qedar
Area: Jerusalem
Population: 450
Established: 1985
Location on map: G10
Latitude: 440
Type: Community Settlement
Planner: The Settlement
Planning Department

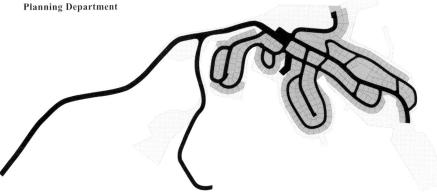

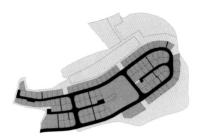

Talmon
Area: Ramallah
Population: 1200
Established: 1989
Location on map: E8
Latitude: 560
Type: Community Settlement
Planner: A. Wilenberg, Gile'adi

→

Zufim
Area: Tul Karem
Population: 850
Established: 1989
Location on map: D5
Latitude: 145
Type: Community Settlement
Planner: Eilon Meromi,
Gertner-Gibor-Koms

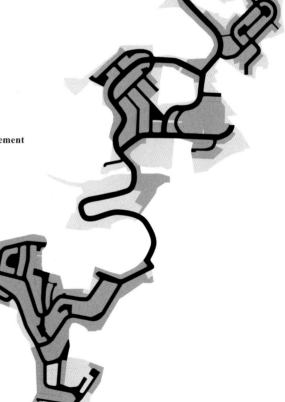

142

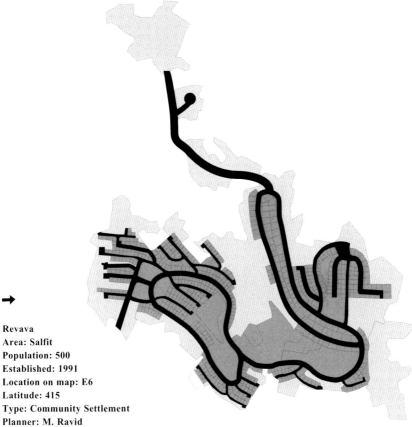

Revava
Area: Salfit
Population: 500
Established: 1991
Location on map: E6
Latitude: 415
Type: Community Settlement
Planner: M. Ravid

Ramat Modi'in
Area: Ramallah
Population: 1800
Established: 1996
Location on map: D8
Latitude: 240
Type: Local Council

143

Mitzpe Yericho, Jericho region
photograph: Efrat Shvily, 1993

next page: Ma'ale Edummim, Greater Jerusalem
photograph: Efrat Shvily, 1993

145

148

Talmon, Ramallah region
photographs: Efrat Shvily, 1993

Ma'ale Edummim, Jerusalem region
photograph: Milutin Labudovic
for Peace Now, 2002

9.

Eran Tamir-Tawil

TO START
A CITY FROM
SCRATCH

AN INTERVIEW WITH ARCHITECT
THOMAS M. LEITERSDORF

T homas Leitersdorf heads a leading architectural and town-planning practice in Tel Aviv. He was educated at the Architectural Association in London and began his career working with Bill Perera in the United States on town-planning projects in Orlando, Florida and in the Ivory Coast, where he planned the expansion of the capital, Abidjan. Leitersdorf returned to Israel in the 1970s, and has since become one of its most influential architects, whose projects within and beyond the Green Line have been widely acclaimed.

Leitersdorf designed two cities in the West Bank, Ma'ale Edummim and Emanuel. Ma'ale Edummim, located east of Jerusalem in the mountains of the Judean Desert, was built by the Israeli government and grew to become the largest Israeli city-settlement in the West Bank. Emanuel,[1] located south-west of Nablus and the first town to be built for the ultra-Orthodox, was one of the largest settlements built by the private sector.

This interview seeks to describe a practitioner's point of view: the professional considerations to be taken into account when building new cities in mountainous regions. The fact that these cities are in effect settlements built in occupied land means that 'professional' considerations have to deal with the political objectives of the state as well as with the security and social realities in the West Bank.

How did you come to work on the planning of Ma'ale Edummim?
When I returned to Israel we began work on the National Masterplan for Tourism with the Minister of Tourism at the time, Gideon Patt. He introduced me to the planning of Ma'ale Edummim.

The strategy in Judea and Samaria at the time was to 'capture ground': you capture as much area as possible by placing few people on numerous hills. The underlying political idea was that the further inside the Occupied Territories we placed settlers, the more territory Israel would have when the time came to set the permanent international borders—because we were already there. This was similar to the strategy employed in Yamit.[2]

Building Ma'ale Edummim right next to Jericho was a government decision, and its location was accurately specified—at the 'end of the desert', the furthest place from Israel that was conceivibly possible.

I was given map co-ordinates and was told to build a town.

'How big?' I asked. 'As big as possible,' I was told.

When I went to see the site I noticed a number of things. The morphology of the area was highly irregular and in order to build a town there you would have had to flatten it entirely. The site was suitable for building nice hilltop villages, but it was not a site for a larger town. In addition, it was climatically suffocating: at the point where the mountains start to rise you get all the winds from the existing industrial area and you can hardly breathe. The decision about Ma'ale Edummim's location was, without doubt, political.

I went back to the minister and told him that to the best of my knowledge this was not a place to build a town. He replied that, with all due respect, this was a government decision and that in one hundred and twenty days the bulldozers had to begin work on the site. I proposed, therefore, to design two alternatives—one where the government wanted the town, and the other where I saw fit. But to do so, I said, would cost the government money. I required a team of consultants that included economists and climate specialists.

Sixty days later I returned to the minister with three alternative sites, including the one proposed by the government. These were rated according to the morphology of the terrain, the climate, accessibility to infrastructure, and proximity to employment centers—the ABC of town planning.

Were these the parameters that you yourself defined?

Yes. No parameters were given to me. All I was told was 'to build a town here'. To persuade the minister, I quantified and qualified the alternatives in terms of cost per housing unit, natural conditions and accessibility. The moment he saw the proposal he was convinced. In fact, it was his idea not to build just another settlement with mobile homes. The idea was to take land that was state land proper and build a city that could compete with any other city in terms of the services and the type of housing it offered. Compared to what went on before, this was revolutionary—as many hills as possible, as far as possible.

When we put the alternatives to the Ministerial Committee for Settlement, headed at the time by Ariel Sharon, the only questions asked were: 'Which of the alternative locations has better control over the main routes?' And 'Which town has a better chance to grow quickly and offer qualities that would make it competitive with Jerusalem?'

I replied that according to these criteria the ideal location would be location A—which lay between the desert and the inhabited land, still benefitted from rain and vegetation and had proximity to existing infrastructure and to an important international route of historical significance, which begins in Jerusalem and passes by Jericho on the way to Amman. At that moment Sharon rose and declared, without consulting the Committee, that 'the State of Israel decides on location A'.

Another problem was that this happened at a time when the United States was exerting pressure on Israel not to build new settlements in Judea and Samaria, and had stationed observers in various places in the Occupied Territories to ensure that nothing happened. But it was also the point at which construction work on the new airports in the Negev Desert, following Israel's withdrawal from Sinai, had finished. The situation was this: the State of Israel wanted a city; true, there was fear of the Americans, but there was a lot of construction equipment standing idle in the desert. One day someone said that the observers had left, and fifteen construction companies together with six big infrastructure companies went up the mountain and erected a city in one go.

In light of these constraints we, the planners, recommended parallel design: while one team was doing the masterplan, I required that they put at my disposal twelve architectural teams that would do the detailed design of the neighborhoods at the same time, before the masterplan was complete. A feedback mechanism was created between myself, as the master planner, and the architects, each of whom wanted to integrate their design into the plan a little differently. By the time the masterplan was complete, all the neighborhoods had already been designed. This meant that all the construction companies could start working at once.

Building a city is like driving a railway engine—it is very heavy when it is static, but once it receives an initial boost it 'takes off'. This never happens if you build a city bit by bit. After all, who is the consumer of the city? Its citizens. And what do they want? They want to have their home, their school, their neighborhood, a synagogue. If you do not provide all these at once you get the dormitory hilltop communities made up of mobile homes, as was the case in the rest of Judea and Samaria at the time.

What was the size of the city that was developed in the initial phase?
It comprised at least two thousand housing units. This was unheard of, because until then a settlement consisted of eight or twelve mobile homes. At this point there was already opposition from the mayor of Jerusalem Teddy Kollek, as he began to see that Ma'ale Edummim would draw population from Jerusalem and compete with it on unequal terms. In contrast to Jerusalem, Ma'ale Edummim was built and subsidized by the government. The government was interested in supporting young couples, so it offered them a higher quality of housing next to Jerusalem, for significantly less money.

In the beginning two types of population came to Ma'ale Edummim: the people who already lived in the temporary settlement in what is known as the Edummim Plain—the 'pioneers'—and people who came from Jerusalem to improve their quality of life.

How did you see Ma'ale Edummim within the metropolitan system of Jerusalem?
We decided to locate the city on the axis that linked Jerusalem and the Dead Sea. As there was already industrial development on the Edummim Plain, we decided that it was a good site in terms of employment. The idea was that the rest of the area should remain open. Ma'ale Edummim lies at the very edge of the desert. The city, therefore, should open up to the view—all the way to the Dead Sea.

Even then we had made the claim that if you want to settle more people you should enlarge the town, instead of building more small settlements. The objective was to leave open spaces by centralizing all new building in existing towns—which is standard practice today. In addition, by concentrating more urban population in one place we were able to provide a higher level and a larger number of services in terms of commerce, amenities, public institutions and facilities.

Did this not run counter to the political demands to take over as much area as possible?
When the government accepted the concept of building one large town instead of a lot of small settlements, we were left to our own devices. Nothing succeeds like success. Ma'ale Edummim was a success story and every apartment that went on the market was instantly grabbed. So

the politicians said, 'OK, the population in Judea and Samaria is growing, we have no marketing problems and we don't have to pay out huge subsidies to support mobile homes on various hills.' We were given free rein because our planning interests were in line with their political interests. I would say that the glory of that time was that the planning and political considerations went hand in hand.

Did you also look at the Arab neighborhoods of Jerusalem?
We quickly realized that the route between Jerusalem and Ma'ale Edummim that went through Azaria and Abu-Dis[3] was a politically unstable connection. Once every few weeks there was a stone-throwing incident. We realized that the only way to strengthen the connection between Ma'ale Edummim and Jerusalem was to create an alternative route that did not go through these neighborhoods. So we proposed the northern road which today links Ma'ale Edummim with Jerusalem and the Dead Sea.

It was a very difficult road to build because of the steep slopes that were involved. But the politicians decided that the Public Works Department's standards for building roads on slopes could handle it due to the importance of the road.

There was one more thing: Ma'ale Edummim in its new location was within the area of Israeli political consensus. The Left at the time, relying on the Allon Plan,[4] as well as the Right, were in accord on the location of Ma'ale Edummim. The Left did not want the settlements at the heart of the Palestinian population, in Nablus or Jenin. The land stretching from Jerusalem to Jericho was state land which Israel had 'inherited' from the Jordanians. These were state lands per se, which was the reason that a consensus on Ma'ale Edummim could be reached—the land was not taken from anyone.

Naturally, the fact that it was within the political consensus greatly helped Ma'ale Edummim. It was not a city of the Right or of the Left, but a city of a consensus.

What was the urban scheme of Ma'ale Edummim?
We did not want to fight nature. At no point did we want to have a retaining wall more than two meters high. This is a mountainous area—its morphology resembled the open palm of a hand. When I

made the first sketch I placed the town center in the 'middle', and the neighborhoods on the 'fingers'. The areas in between—the valleys—remained open and untouched, leading directly to the heart of the town. The houses were terraced, without pilotis, and all the pedestrian routes connected to the green areas without crossing the main roads. It was a very simple scheme—a ring, with those living inside it never having to cross the internal roads. This created a very safe environment for children.

What made the buildings in Ma'ale Edummim unique at the time?
We used climate specialists and set up climate measuring stations. This was considered revolutionary. At the time the whole of the State of Israel looked like Holon and Bat Yam—apartment blocks of four stories on pilotis. One of the recommendations of our climate specialists was not to build on pilotis but on the ground—this was because of the winds. The Ministry of Housing was very skeptical on this point and said that it could not get a good price for ground-floor flats. We said the opposite—if you raise the ground floor about a meter off the ground, it sits above the road but it allows you to provide the ground floor with a garden. You give better conditions than the first floor. Today everybody does it, but then—it was a novelty. It was a battle, but as it was a new town they decided to experiment. They conducted the experiment and, of course, the proof of the pudding is in the eating—the flats with the little garden in front sold best.

How did you deal with the issue of view?
In Ma'ale Edummim we have two views: the scenery of Jerusalem with its towers, and the distant view towards the Dead Sea and the mountains of Edom. We had to take care to preserve these views because this is what we were selling. We were selling something that did not cost us a penny; all we had to do was be careful and not do anything stupid that would hide the view that was already there.

Were you also involved in choosing the site for Emanuel?
Choosing the site for Emanuel was an entertaining process. A group of ultra-Orthodox developers came to me with a 1:50,000 map, with six points marked on it, each measuring two or three hectares, and they told

me that they wanted to build a town. I did not take them very seriously—but if someone comes into your office you don't throw them out. So I took their map and said, 'What you have shown me is not a town.' Then they asked, 'What do you need for a town?' So with a 6B pencil I drew on the map what the size of a town should be, and they told me, 'It's yours, start planning.'

That is how it was. I started planning and they went and checked who owned all the parcels of land. Part of the land belonged to Arabs who lived in Jordan and London, so they simply went out and bought it from them. By the time I had finished planning they had finished buying, more or less according to the circle I had drawn. I still did not take them seriously. I wanted to discourage them so I drew them a circle, but what could I do if they came back with the circle?

How did the work on the planning of Emanuel develop?
The situation in Emanuel was that you had young developers who had no money. They had no money to make a survey of the area, and certainly no money for traffic planners and the like. So they came to me and told me, 'Design a city, but you have to know that we have no money for anything.' So instead of sending surveyors to the site we took large-scale maps and enlarged them to the scale of 1:1,000. As we were not road engineers we decided that we would simply lay the roads on the natural morphology, that we would not change the mountains at all. It was as if you were to take a topographic line from the map and make a road on it—that is how it was built.

As the slopes in Emanuel are much steeper than those of Ma'ale Edummim, we developed buildings that could work on steeper slopes, with the building itself acting as a retaining wall. The stepped building supports the slope while the road accurately follows the contour of the topography. The result was that we achieved very cheap construction because we did not have to pay for retaining walls.

In the beginning Emanuel was a great success, like Ma'ale Edummim. It provided a solution for all the young ultra-Orthodox couples that could not afford the prices in Bnei Brak,[5] which is one of the most expensive cities in Israel. The ultra-Orthodox population has special needs and cannot live anywhere like you and me.

As the land was purchased relatively cheaply, and the

government helped by subsidizing the infrastructure, the developers were able to offer apartments priced at a quarter of what you would pay in Bnei Brak or Jerusalem. It was initially a great success. Its downfall came when a few businessmen put their hands in the till. Until this happened, though, the city experienced a meteoric rise. We ourselves built more than 1,500 apartments.

What was the urban concept of Emanuel?
By and large we once again took the morphology we had and on it we built the town in the most fitting and cost-effective way—we had no money for landscaping in Emanuel.

How was the architecture of Emanuel determined?
On the one hand, the morphology of the area dictated the stepped buildings and the retaining walls, while, on the other, the architecture was determined by the specific needs of the population, characterized by religious requirements combined with limited resources and large families. This means that you have to design rooms that will house four or five children. The basic module of a room is the bed and you have to arrange it wisely, like in a submarine, one bed on top, or next to the other. The design is to an entirely different standard, as each apartment has to have a special sink for Passover as well as a second sink for everyday use, and each apartment has to have a balcony open to the sky for a Sukkah.[6] That was the story of Emanuel.

We have three examples of cities you built from scratch, or almost from scratch—Abidjan in the Ivory Coast and Ma'ale Edummim and Emanuel in Israel. Are there any similarities in the design?
In the Ivory Coast we were dealing with the design of a city, which on the one hand had to serve the French and the other European communities as well as tourists, while on the other it had to relate to the traditional African villages in the area and needed to remain there.

In Abidjan, when the commercial center sits next to an existing village, it does not touch it. This allows for the necessary accessibility and provides the village with the possibility of growing and developing, while retaining the existing separation. People like to meet out of choice, not because someone forces them to. This is the principle we applied. In

Abidjan there are two communities that need to cohabit, whereas in Emanuel there is a distinctively homogeneous community.

Did the Arab villages that can be seen in the area influence your architecture?
I look upon the morphology of the Arab villages with envy. The beauty of the Arab village lies in its accumulative and somewhat irrational nature—development progresses slowly, with each generation adding on to the existing fabric built by its predecessor.

Our approach, on the other hand, determined by the government, produces an instant city. In three years we churned out a couple of thousand apartments—all built on one concept, one system of construction and infrastructure. For them it is different. In the beginning there was a donkey track. A man builds a home, a son is born, the son gets married and they need to add something, so they add it on to the area of the street. But so long as there is still room enough for the donkey, there is no room for the car and all that it entails. But if you look at this process logically, by today's standards, you can't build a city this way. You can't pass up the necessary infrastructure or traffic and you can't provide a minimum level of services. But in terms of beauty they are way ahead of us!

Architecture without architects—this is the Arab village, and this is its beauty. It is always better than when an architect comes in; the architect only spoils things because the architect has to work logically, and they do not.

From the political perspective and from the perspective of their urban development, how do you see Ma'ale Edummim and Emanuel today?
I think that the fact that Ma'ale Edummim was created by a government decision and within the national political consensus gave it great strength that helped it through the years.

Ma'ale Edummim is also an excellent example of the great importance of the government bringing a city to a take-off threshold quickly. This was the strength of Ma'ale Edummim and the weakness of Emanuel. Emanuel was given the initial push but it didn't manage to take off before someone put his hand on the cash.

As to the politics of Jews and Arabs, I cannot contribute because I am very weak on politics. To tell you that an architect influences politics? He doesn't. The whole story of Judea and Samaria could have been different, but this is on levels that are neither in your hands nor mine.

The interview was conducted at Thomas Leitersdorf's
office in Tel Aviv, April 2002

notes:

1. 'Judea and Samaria' is the preferred term used by the Israeli Right and the settlers for the West Bank. The Israeli Left and the Palestinians, on the other hand, prefer the use of the term 'Occupied Territories', which also includes the Gaza Strip. (Leitersdorf uses both terms in the conversation.)
2. Yamit was an Israeli town built in Sinai and eventually evacuated in 1982 following the peace treaty with Egypt.
3. Azaria and Abu-Dis are two Arab neighborhoods in East Jerusalem on the road connecting Jerusalem to Ma'ale Edummim.
4. The Allon Plan was proposed by the Israeli Minister Yigal Allon (1967). Its basic premise was that Israel should settle only in areas with sparse Palestinian population.
5. Bnei Brak is a city near Tel Aviv inhabited mainly by ultra-Orthodox Jews.
6. The Sukkah is a temporary structure erected during the Jewish festival of Sukkot and which has to be open to the sky.

10.

Nadav Harel

AREA K
STILLS FROM THE FILM AREA K
GAZA STRIP, 2000

Dugit, Israeli fishing village established 1990

for the kids it's the best place to grow up

it's a classic place to grow up

this is my new 400 sqm. house

It's like living in a construction site

for security, the army flattened down the Palestinian orange groves

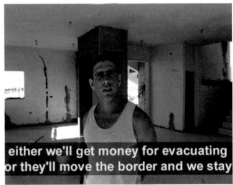

either we'll get money for evacuating or they'll move the border and we stay

nobody comes to visit us anymore

we saw it from the living room,
the army killed a terrorist

11.

Gideon Levy

THE LOWEST POINTS IN ISRAEL

page 166: Bulldozer, Halhul Bypass, Hebron Region
photograph: Miki Kratsman, 1996

The lowest points in Israel are to be found, of all places, on the mountain peaks and hilltops. It is no mere chance that the settlements built by Israel in the territories it has occupied have positioned themselves on these lofty heights. The settlements are almost always up there, scarring the landscape, dominating the plateau, challenging, provoking, picking a fight. Down in the flatlands live the 'natives'—the Palestinians, who built their houses in order to live in them, not in order to taunt and defy and provoke hatred. The settlers up above, the Palestinians down below—this is the essence of the story. In the spring of 2002 you cannot drive along the roads of the West Bank for more than a few minutes without catching sight of them towering above you. In the spring of 2002 you can hardly find a window in a Palestinian house that does not open on to the red-tiled roofs or orange-tinted security lighting of the neighboring settlement. Neighboring? You can find everything over there—everything but neighbors. One beside the other, two communities living in hatred and fear of each other. One on top, armed with tanks, roadblocks and helicopters, the other below, armed only with their steadfast hold on the land. Which is stronger? And which will survive?

Only he who is not convinced of the justness of his way, his genuine connection to the land, the degree to which his hold on the land is legal, his own integrity, only he has the need to build in such a provocative, forceful manner, placing his house on the top of the hill and relying on so much force in order to stay there. Behind the barbed-wire fence (and the latest addition: electrified fences—yes, electrified fences, with all their connotations), behind roadblocks manned by armed soldiers and security officers, behind floodlights and iron gates, behind sandbags and concrete blocks, in vehicles armored against stones—and lately against gunfire—driven by civilians who are almost always armed, and in buses escorted by jeeps and troops of soldiers, the settlers go about their business in a land that is not their own, filled with people who don't want them there. The children go to ballet and clarinet classes accompanied by armed guards, and the elderly drive to their weekly game of bridge with a rifle stuck between their knees. More than a few of them have already been killed; many more of us await our death because of the settlers' whims.

From the window of a burnt clothing store in re-occupied Bethlehem, from a bathroom window in Kafr Beth-Dajan, from a living room window in the village of Sinjel, from the mouth of a cave belonging to the cave-dwellers in southern Mount Hebron, from an office in Nablus, from a store in Ramallah—from everywhere you can spot the settlement on the hilltop, looming, threatening, dreadfully colonial. Ganim and Kasdim over Jenin, Psagot over Ramallah, Ariel over Salfit, Elon Moreh over the Askar refugee camp, Ma'ale Edummim over Azariyah, Beitar Ilit over Nahalin, Bracha over Borin, Yizhar over Hawara: alienated, threatening, conquering houses, lusting for more. The breaching of the international law that explicitly prohibits the transfer of civilian population into occupied territory—an act that is considered a war crime by the Fourth Geneva Convention—is overlooked by Israel. International law? The Geneva Convention? Not for the Israelis, who willfully ignore the legal aspects of the settlements. America and Russia, China and Japan, France and Germany, Egypt and Morocco, Chad and Sri Lanka—what other issues summon such complete agreement? Nevertheless, Israel holds its own.

Living by their swords, some 200,000 Israelis crowd into the backyard of their country, risking not only their own lives and the lives of their children, but also those of all Israelis who have found themselves caught up in an escalating spiral of violence caused by this settlement craze. And no one is asking them to account for it. Some of these bandits seized the land illegally in the dead of night, and no one has dared evacuate them. Others settled with the support of various Israeli governments, who have all had—with no exceptions—one thing in common: they endorsed this grotesque enterprise. The 'Man of Peace', Ehud Barak, built no less than 6,045 residential units in the Occupied Territories during the twenty months he was in office. While presuming to bring an end to the Israeli-Palestinian conflict, he built at the same rate as his predecessor, the reactionary right-wing prime minister, Yitzhak Shamir. The dovish politician Yigal Allon came up with the idea for Kiryat Arba—another mega-settlement—and Shimon Peres, the Nobel Peace Prize Laureate, was the initiator of Elon Moreh. All this, without even mentioning the leaders endeared to the settlers: Ariel Sharon, Yisrael Galili, Menachem Begin and Moshe Dayan. Right-wing and left-wing sing the tune of the settlements in perfect unison.

In his book *Guide to an Injured Dove*, former minister Yossi Beilin laments his sin: the Israelis, he says, including himself, never understood how devastating the settlement enterprise is for the Palestinian people, the people with whom Beilin and his colleagues were striving to attain a peace agreement. 'When will you Israelis understand that nothing scares us more than the settlements?' Marwan Barghouti, the man who later became the leader of the Tanzim (the military wing of Yassir Arafat's Fatah faction), asked me back in 1997 while we were driving down a West Bank road. And it is true: most Israelis never actually realized the meaning of these horribly ugly concrete blocks constructed by their country on Palestinian land. In the mean time, the monster that has taken shape over the last thirty-five years of occupation has long since realized the objective of its creators; it has indeed become the most difficult obstacle along the way to a peace agreement with the Palestinian people. The mere fact that the settlements exist on the land—the last piece of land left as a refuge for the Palestinians after their tragedy in 1948—transforms every house into an obstacle to peace.

It is not difficult to imagine what would have happened if the settlements had not been established; how the territorial aspect of the conflict would be so easy to resolve, how it would simply dissolve into thin air, and how the only just borders, those of June 1967, would have easily become Israel's international borders, thereby separating it from the small Palestinian state and perhaps even enabling peaceful relations. But the land of the Palestinians, the narrow strip of land they have left of their, and our, 'promised land', has turned into the land of the settlements. And so we find them up there, on the mountaintops—the lowest points in Israel: immoral, unjust, reeking of war.

Take, for example, the Beth El settlement. Most Israelis have never visited such a mega-settlement. They have no clue as to what a resident of this settlement sees when he opens the window of his home. To the east, the settler from Beth El sees only troops. The access road to his settlement now crosses a colossal army base, the headquarters of the many troops required to guard the settlement and its surroundings. The way home passes tanks and storerooms of rifles and ammunition (which should probably legally not be there). To the west, the settler from Beth El sees an abandoned highway strewn with rocks and dirt roadblocks. This is the old road connecting Ramallah and Nablus, the Palestinian highway that has fallen into neglect ever since Israel prohibited its use. If the settler looks a little further, he will be able to make out small yellow marks on the sides of the road. These are Palestinian taxis driving down dirt paths, transporting the handful of villagers who have succeeded in bypassing the numerous roadblocks on foot. In wind and in rain, in all kinds of weather, they meander around the roadblocks; they have no other choice. To the north, at the low point of the abandoned highway, a large group of wretched houses crowd within a fence that encircles them as if in a jail. This is the home of some six thousand Palestinians, residents of the Jilazun refugee camp, who have been imprisoned for several months. Sometimes, they find ways to escape on foot through the valleys, but this carries the risk of being shot at by soldiers—a quite likely possibility that has already come about more than once. Leaving the camp by car is not an option. These hopeless people who have been dealt two blows by fate—one in 1948, and another in 1967—have now suffered a third: their freedom of movement and employment have been taken away. Trapped in their miserable camp, they can only raise their eyes to gaze bitterly at the mega-settlement that has sprung up before their eyes, bountiful and spacious.

To the south of Jilazun, the settler can make out the Surda roadblock, where an Israeli soldier was killed not long ago while protecting his settlement. Further southwest, albeit out of sight, is the extensively fortified Ein Ariq roadblock where six IDF soldiers, stationed at the outpost in order to protect a handful of settlers in the Dolav and Talmon settlements (neighbors of the Beth El settler), were killed. Further northwest is the campus of Bir-Zeit University, where the dreams of thousands of youths—no different from the dreams of the youths of Beth El—to gain an education and a profession, have faded away. The university closes and reopens sporadically, and studies during the last two years have been completely disrupted because of the roadblocks and the war. When students are able to attend their university, it is only on foot.

Looking to the east, near the military court and the base, the settler will be able to discern a long line of Palestinian villagers walking silently alongside the fences, in the shadow of the tanks. Children and the elderly, pregnant women and sick patients carry their bags as the turret of a tank throws its threatening shadow upon them. These are the residents of the nearby villages who have no other way of reaching their regional town, Ramallah, other than on foot. They walk six or seven kilometers in each direction in order to get to work, to stores or to the clinic. The settlers' cars cruise by on the bypass road open only to Jews.

Tanks, roadblocks, refugees, bypass roads, columns of villagers on foot, ambulances driving haphazardly down improvised dirt paths— a great and awesome suffering is the view that the settler from Beth El sees every day from his window, and he remains indifferent.

It's difficult to understand how, among some 200,000 settlers, there is not one person who has the integrity to stand up and admit that his settlement, along with all the others, is causing all this pain and suffering. It's Sodom without a single righteous man. An immense degree of wickedness is required to take away from the Palestinians their last piece of land, to occupy it so crudely and to say: everything, absolutely everything is ours, because we are stronger, because we have the power to take it.

A bypass near Nablus
photograph: Miki Kratsman, 2002

174

These stills are taken from a video documentary
by a Palestinian human rights activist who
prefers to remain anonymous. It describes the work
of an Israeli army bulldozer destroying the
infrastructure and blocking a road in Bethlehem
during Operation 'Defensive Shield', April 2002.

The Salem checkpoint, Jenin region
photograph: Pavel Wolberg, 2002

176

next page: **Itamar, Nablus region**
photograph: **Pavel Wolberg, 2002**

Erecting fortifications near the settlement
of Eli, Ramallah region
photograph: Pavel Wolberg, 2001

Barkan, Salfit region
photograph: Pavel Wolberg, 2001

next page: Balata refugee camp,
a view from Mount Gerizim
photograph: Pavel Wolberg, 2002

12.

Meron Benvenisti

IN THE LIGHT OF THE MORNING AFTER

Few are the landscapes that arouse sadness and compassion like those from which the human component has been uprooted, and where only the physical framework created by the absentees in their own form and image remains. The world is full of these landscapes: Algeria, Asia Minor, Israel/Palestine, India/Pakistan, Indochina, Kenya, Eastern Prussia, Silesia, the Sudeten region as well as the former Yugoslavia—places abandoned following wars, riots and collapsed colonial regimes. People either escaped or were banished, carrying with them only their personal belongings. They left behind their homes, places of worship, ancestors' graves and their unique material culture: from agrarian cultivation to settlement patterns, from church belfries to inscriptions carved in stone immortalizing forgotten events in foreign tongues.

Relics of the waning past refuse to disappear. Wherever you may look, you come across the signposts of a lost civilization in the remains of which lives another, different people that adjusted the remains to their own needs and tastes. In the process, signs of the past are ignored and the unique cultural characteristics of the uprooted are wilfully demolished as the fears grow that these may later serve claims for return.

The visitor then observes the structures and ponders the human tragedy that has remained frozen in carved stone: in a bedroom turned shop, a temple turned restaurant and in an inscription that has been blurred. Israeli writer S. Yizhar describes an Arab village deserted during the war of 1948 thus:

'And suddenly, in mid-afternoon or just before evening, the village—which only a moment before had been just a few desolate, silent, orphaned hovels, heavy silence, and the wail of heart-rending laments—this large and gloomy village opens up and sings a song of belongings whose breath has departed; a song of human deeds that have been reduced to their elements and run wild; a song bringing bad tidings of sudden calamity, which freezes and remains suspended like a curse that does not cross the lips, and fear … and a flash, here and there a kind of flash of revenge, of a challenge to fight, of a "God of Vengeance, appear!" … walls that somebody had toiled to decorate the best he could … an orderliness that was understood by someone and disorder that one could sort out … rags that are familiar to those who are accustomed to them. Ways of life that have unravelled, their meaning lost … and a great, all-pervading muteness; resting on the love and the noise. And the trouble and the hope, and the pleasant hours and the unpleasant—they are all corpses that will not be buried.

'And here are the checkerboard fields, ploughed and turning green, and the deeply shaded orchards, and the hedges that dissect the area in tranquil patterns ...—and behold, the grief of orphanhood is descending on all of them like an opaque bridal veil. Fields that will not be harvested. Orchards that will not be watered. Paths that will be desolate. And a kind of loss—and twas all for naught. Thorns and brambles straggling over everything. And a parched yellowness, the wail of the wilderness ...'[1]

Sometimes the landscape is abandoned and becomes desolate, but more often than not the deserted landscape rapidly fills with another people who look upon the relics of the past as a mere nuisance and whose lives amidst the ruins compel 'adjustments' of eradication and new construction. And slowly, or with resolute effort, a new human layer of existence is formed upon the old one and mingles with it.

The new people evolve to become entrenched natives themselves. The inherited and transformed landscape becomes their homeland, whilst the affinity of the uprooted to their ancestral land becomes a challenge to the very existence of the settlers.

There are places where reconciliation has been attained between the altered human landscape and the physical one, frozen or transformed, where past traumas retreat into nostalgia. There are, however, places where eviction and settlement continue to serve as cries for battle and the physical landscape becomes a theater of war, in which the environment and cultural values are sacrificed on the altar of aggressive existential confrontation. Political and ideological decisions shape the physical environment, while patriotism—the refuge of the villain, the charlatan and the glutton—conceals the foolishness, the damage and the environmental destruction. As the years go by, the affluent and powerful party enforces its material culture, while the remaining defeated party mimics its buildings and settlements. Furthermore, embedded within the arrogance of the victors there exists an obvious component of hubris—a repudiation of world order and an arrogant challenge against the Gods. And for this sin of hubris the Gods mete out heavy punishment.

It is distressing to see a landscape abandoned by its human

element. But disturbing and more tragic still is the sight of built and flourishing settlements crowded by people and full of activity, knowing that sooner or later, but inevitably, the settlers will be displaced. This is the emotional response to the sight of Jewish settlements in the West Bank and the Gaza Strip, in the heart of a dense Palestinian population. The perception on which the Jewish Settlement Project in the Occupied Territories was founded was that of the eternal weakness and inferiority of the Palestinians. Those who built the settlements presumed that the Palestinians would remain forever submissive and obsequious. How else would it be possible to explain the reasoning behind the establishment of Jewish islands in the heart of an Arab population? The victor's vanity, self-righteousness and the feeling of superiority—bordering on racism—that was at the source of its aggressive incursion into the homogeneous Palestinian fabric. The assumption was that millions of people would forever agree to the existence of a domineering minority amongst them. And when the error became apparent, and the Palestinians began to rebel, the inevitable countdown towards the eviction of the arrogant settlements upon the hilltops commenced.

It is impossible to predict how tomorrow will look, when it will come and how. In peace or violence? Will the Jewish settlements be evacuated peacefully and handed over to the Palestinian refugees? Will they be destroyed following violent resistance or will they prevail? And on which terms: peaceful coexistence or their military superiority?

The future of the settlements is currently perceived in terms of a political solution in accordance with a rational and optimistic model, which views the Israeli-Palestinian conflict as a national-ethnic conflict, the solution to which is 'two states for two peoples'. However, it is possible that this model was never viable, or that there were strong forces that succeeded in destroying it. Or, possibly, that the fundamental hostility between the settlers that struck roots and the natives that were expelled or subjugated does not allow for the attainment of mutual recognition and equal rights. This is why a solution of separation on the basis of equality is not viable, since in reality there exists a de facto bi-national entity. The only option, therefore, is to think in terms of a single geopolitical unit, in which two rival communities reside in perpetual enmity. In this context some settlements will remain in place, and others will be evacuated due to insecure living conditions.

Either way, with or without deliberate destruction, the retreating settlers will be tormented by the tragedy of evacuation, and the physical environment will suffer a traumatic transformation. Should the departing Israelis not destroy the settlements, Palestinians will inhabit them and will probably adjust the structures to the own physical and cultural needs, with numerous alterations.

Though the human landscape may be exchanged, the results of mass building are irreversible. The Israeli settlements generated extreme changes in the physical environment of the Occupied Territories, the most pronounced example of which is Ma'ale Edummim, the Israeli construction in the desert between Jerusalem and Jericho. The town, with its adjoining Jewish settlements, forms a sweeping built-up area that entirely blurs the dramatic confrontation between the desert and the planted land. The significance of Jerusalem as a city perched on the border between the arid barren land and the fertile populated land—a confrontation that has always defined the physical and historic environment of the Holy City—has been destroyed for ever. No change in the human landscape will rescind this physical change. Irreversible, too, is the extensive environmental damage caused by the hysterical paving of bypass roads built as a result of the temporary and erroneous considerations of security measures. The arrogance of the founders of the Jewish Settlement Project will not disappear, and neither will those who perpetuated it. It is immortalised in the hundreds of thousands of tons of concrete that bury the hills of the West Bank beneath them.

notes:

1. S. Yizhar, *Khirbet Hiza'a*, Tel Aviv: Zmora Bitan, 1989, pp. 47, 68 (Hebrew). English translation by Maxine Kaufman-Lacusta.

right: **Ofra, and the Palestinian village of a-Taibeh, Ramallah region**
photograph: **Milutin Labudovic for Peace Now, 2002**

BIOGRAPHIES:

Daniel Bauer is a photographer based in Tel Aviv whose work has been exhibited internationally. He teaches photography at Bezalel Academy of Arts and Design in Jerusalem.

Meron Benvenisti was the deputy mayor of Jerusalem from 1971 to 1978 and is currently a columnist for *Haaretz*. He is the author of *Conflicts and Contradictions* (1986), *Intimate Enemies* (California University Press, 1995), *City of Stone* (California University Press, 1996), and *Sacred Landscape* (California University Press, 2000).

Zvi Efrat is a partner in Efrat-Kowalsky Architects and the head of the Architecture Department at Bezalel Academy of Arts and Design in Jerusalem. He curated the exhibitions *The Israeli Project* (Tel Aviv Museum, 2000) and *Borderline Disorder* (the Israeli Pavilion at the Venice Biennale, 2002).

Nadav Harel is a film-maker working in Tel Aviv and New York. His films have been broadcast on national television networks in Israel and abroad, and have won many awards in international film festivals.

Miki Kratsman is a photographer based in Tel Aviv. He works for the local Tel Aviv newspaper *Ha'ir* and has collaborated with Gideon Levy at *Haaretz* since 1995. He teaches photography at the College for Management, University of Haifa and at Vital School of Design in Tel Aviv.

Milutin Labudovic emigrated to Israel from Belgrade in 2001, where he worked as a photographer for the weekly *Ilustrovana Politika* and the daily *Vecerne Novosti*. Milutin currently works as a freelance photographer for Peace Now.

Gideon Levy is a columnist for *Haaretz*, head of the Journalism Department at the Camera Obscura School of Arts and a former aide to Shimon Peres.

Ilan Potash is an architect working in Tel Aviv. He is a former student of Rafi Segal at the Technion in Haifa.

Sharon Rotbard is an architect practicing in Tel Aviv. He is the editor of the architectural series at Babel and is currently writing a book entitled *The Architecture of the Possible: Avraham Yaski and the Israeli Adrihalut*.

Rafi Segal established his own architectural practice in 2000 after working in partnership with Zvi Hecker on the design of the Palmach Museum in Tel Aviv. His theoretical and practical work has gained him the Young Artist Award and later the Young Architect Prize from the Israel Association of United Architects.

Efrat Shvily is a journalist and photographer based in Jerusalem. Her work has been published and exhibited internationally.

Eran Tamir-Tawil is an architect based in Tel Aviv. He is a former research assistant to Eyal Weizman.

David Tartakover is an Israeli communication designer, artist and curator who specializes in Israeli culture and politics. He is member of AGI (Alliance Graphique Internationale) and is the Israel Prize Laureate for Design, 2002.

Eyal Weizman is an architect based in Tel Aviv and London who has also co-authored a human rights report and conducted a map-making project for the human rights organization B'Tselem. He is currently developing his doctoral thesis *The Politics of Verticality/ Architecture and Occupation in the West Bank and Gaza* at the *London Consortium* into a film and a book. (www.opendemocracy.net)

Pavel Wolberg is a photographer based in Tel Aviv. He works for *Haaretz* covering mainly military issues. His exhibition *Israel–Point Blank*, curated by Moshe Ninio, opened at the Tel Aviv Museum of Art, 2002.

Oren Yiftachel chairs the Department of Geography at Ben-Gurion University in Beer Sheva, Israel. He teaches political geography and public policy and is a research fellow at the Negev Center for Regional Development. His main research interests critically explore the links between ethno-national politics and the transformation of human space.